PERSIAN GULF WAR

Revised Edition

AMERICA AT WAR

AMERICA AT WAR

PERSIAN GULF WAR

Revised Edition

RODNEY P. CARLISLE

JOHN S. BOWMAN
general editor

CHELSEA HOUSE
PUBLISHERS
An imprint of Infobase Publishing

Persian Gulf War, Revised Edition

Copyright © 2010, 2003 by Rodney P. Carlisle

Maps copyright © 2010, 2003 by Facts On File

Chelsea House Publishers
132 West 31st Street
New York NY 10001

Library of Congress Cataloging-in-Publication Data

Carlisle, Rodney P.
Persian Gulf War / by Rodney Carlisle ; John S. Bowman, general editor. — Rev. ed.
p. cm.
Includes bibliographical references and index.
ISBN 978-0-8160-8192-9 (hc : alk. paper) 1. Persian Gulf War, 1991.
I. Bowman, John Stewart, 1931– II. Title.

DS79.72.C36 2010
956.7044'2—dc22   2009030844

Text design by Erika K. Arroyo
Cover design by Takeshi Takahashi
Composition by Hermitage Publishing Services
Cover printed by Bang Printing, Brainerd, Minn.
Book printed and bound by Bang Printing, Brainerd, Minn.
Date printed: September 2010
Printed in the United States of America

10 9 8 7 6 5 4 3 2 1

This book is printed on acid-free paper.

Contents

Preface

In August 1990, the president of Iraq, Saddam Hussein, ordered his army to invade Kuwait, a small country at the northwestern end of the Persian Gulf. This gulf (also known as the Arabian Gulf) separates the Arabian Peninsula from the main landmass of southwestern Asia. This book examines the United States's special role in the Persian Gulf War of 1990 to 1991 that took place in the wake of Hussein's invasion.

Both Iraq and Kuwait are members of the United Nations, and despite a long-standing claim by Iraq that Kuwait is an Iraqi province, no other countries recognize that claim. It was the first time in history that one member state of the United Nations invaded and conquered another member nation.

The world was shocked. Although both countries were rich from oil, Iraq had poured much of its wealth into building a strong military. Kuwait, on the other hand, was a peaceful, small nation that had used its oil revenue to provide a better life for its citizens in services such as health care and education. The brutal takeover was important for other reasons, however.

If Hussein could take Kuwait without effective resistance, there would be little to stop him from seizing further territory in Saudi Arabia and in other small oil-producing countries along the Persian Gulf. If Kuwait were the first step in a chain of conquests, soon more than half of the entire world's known oil reserves would be under his control. Maps and charts in this book help trace such factors, show resources, and clarify the location of events. But beyond this regional conflict, Hussein's actions confronted Americans with issues that go to the very heart of the United States's role in the world in the 21st century.

It seemed, in 1990, that Iraq suddenly challenged the peaceful new world order that was emerging as the Soviet Union and the United

In the period of coalition-building before attacking Iraq's forces in Kuwait, President George H. W. Bush meets with Jabir al-Ahmad al-Sabah, emir of Kuwait, at the White House, where they wave at photographers in a show of unity. *(George Bush Presidential Library)*

States settled their differences. America took the lead in resisting a further attack into Arabia, and then in liberating Kuwait from its conqueror. This book places that leadership against several different backgrounds.

One background has to do with America's own traditions. The United States had used its armed forces as a "world policeman" in the past, fighting pirates, bandits, guerrillas, insurgents, revolutionaries, and terrorists. But recent history had made Americans reluctant to commit troops overseas. The long, drawn-out Vietnam War, in which more than 58,000 Americans had died, had soured the public on an overseas commitment, it seemed. Public fear of U.S. casualties could stand in the way of helping Kuwait and of serving once again as world policeman. Knowing of this reluctance to intervene, Hussein calculated that the United States would do nothing.

But history showed that Americans would back up a decision to use military force in one of the world's trouble spots under certain conditions. When Americans saw their principles of international law and order challenged, and when they also believed their national self-interest was at stake, they rose to the challenge. It is because of such issues and their possible impact on future actions that this otherwise "minor" war repays study.

Other backgrounds that this account examines are the geography, religion, and politics of the region. The politics of Arab and Muslim brotherhood stood as a possible obstacle to helping Kuwait. As an Arabic and mostly Muslim people, Iraqis were seen as brothers and sisters by the Persian Gulf Arab states. Unless the United States could find allies among other Arabs, it would seem that the United States was simply acting like the European colonial powers of the past, attempting to dictate to non-European peoples how to run their affairs. Without Arab support, a U.S.-led alliance would seem to be neocolonialist imperialism. Religion, too, played a part. As a country with a Christian majority, the United States seemed alien to the Islamic people of the region. Furthermore, with its small but prominent Jewish minority and its strong commitment to maintaining the nation of Israel, the United States was often perceived as an intruder in the Middle East.

Still another background is the history of Iraq itself. The book shows how Iraq built its army and its weapons of mass destruction, and how it fought a long war with neighboring Iran. Saddam Hussein emerged as a ruthless dictator. According to legends that he did not deny, he had personally murdered officers and other government officials who opposed him, and he had ordered the killing of many more. In the war with Iran, he had used poison gas against both Iranian troops and Iraqi civilians who opposed his regime.

The invasion by Iraq of Kuwait was not a simple matter of troops moving in and occupying strategic points. Instead, the Iraqi soldiers looted, raped, and destroyed. They rounded up suspected resisting Kuwaitis and shot them on the spot. As refugees fled Kuwait, many were robbed and others torn from their cars and shot in front of their families. When those who escaped gathered in Egypt and other places, they told their stories and the world learned of one shocking atrocity after another.

Against these backgrounds, the book shows how U.S. president George H. W. Bush worked with his military and diplomatic advisers to construct a broad alliance, or what became known as the Coalition, of countries to come to the defense of Saudi Arabia in what became known as Operation Desert Shield and to liberate Kuwait in what became known as Operation Desert Storm. Different countries took different tasks in the alliance, and some remained on the verge of

During their visit to Saudi Arabia over Thanksgiving weekend in 1990, President and Mrs. Bush met with U.S. and Saudi troops at an air base. *(DOD Defense Information Center, March ARB, California)*

dropping out. However, several Arab countries recognized that opposing Iraq was in their interests and even supplied military help.

Some nations provided only financial aid. Billions of dollars to finance the effort came from countries such as Japan and Korea that depended on the oil supplies from the Persian Gulf region. Other countries in the Coalition, even including some that had once been part of the Soviet sphere of influence in Eastern Europe, sent small units to assist in mine-clearing or in medical work. Egypt, Saudi Arabia, Syria, and smaller Arab states such as Bahrain, Qatar, Oman, and the United Arab Emirates provided troops.

The United States, France, Britain, and Saudi Arabia provided aircraft and pilots. Ships from many nations aided U.S. naval ships. Some, such as Spain and Portugal, restricted their navies to enforcing the blockade of Iraq. But U.S. and British aircraft carriers and missile cruisers participated in the long bombardment of Iraq. By January

1991, the Coalition was strong enough to demand that Iraq withdraw or face attack. When the deadline passed, the air-strike phase of Operation Desert Storm began on January 16, 1991.

As brief and confined as the Gulf War turned out to be, it has become important to study because of several issues that it raised. Many of these issues seem likely to confront Americans for some time to come. One such is the question of the public's right to know just what is taking place in the actual combat zones. During the Vietnam War, some 20 years earlier, world television audiences saw the conflict up close, in their living rooms. In 1991, that television coverage was even more thorough. But during the Persian Gulf War, the military sought to control the flow of information in new ways. A classic conflict of freedom and security played out in every news briefing, press conference, and roll of released film footage.

Another issue increasingly confronting Americans is the status of women in the military during wartime. The Persian Gulf War was the first American war in which American women fought alongside men at the front. With women serving as helicopter pilots and in other roles, the war tested whether the decision to integrate men and women into military units was practical and workable.

Women served in new and frontline roles in the U.S. military during the Gulf War. One such was Lt. Kathy Hambleton, a navigator assigned to refuel aircraft during Operation Desert Shield. *(Defense Imagery)*

Yet another issue is what has come to be known as "collateral damage"—in particular, the accidental wounding or killing of civilians. The air attacks on Iraq blew up more than soldiers and their equipment. In six weeks of bombing and missile attacks, military and civilian targets all over Iraq were destroyed, including secret facilities for the development of nuclear weapons, poison gas, missiles, and long-range artillery. But inevitably, the bombs and missiles killed or injured many innocent civilians.

As the Coalition bombs and missiles pounded Iraq, the Coalition wavered. At home, Americans were fascinated yet horrified by the destruction their new weapons brought to the Iraqi people. Precise, laser-guided bombs seemed impersonal and tidy, like some new video game. But it did not take much imagination to realize that every detonation brought terrible agony, injury, and death to those in its path. In Europe and in the Arabic-speaking world, the public and political leaders began to question the morality of such destruction. Iraqis made use of the media too, leading camera crews to tragic scenes of civilian casualties.

This book explains how the Coalition worked through its doubts and then entered the ground phase of Operation Desert Storm, sending tanks, armored personnel carriers, and foot soldiers against the Iraqi defenses. This phase, which began with frontal attacks of forces into Iraq and occupied Kuwait, started on Sunday, February 24, 1991. The war pitted high-technology U.S. weapons and Coalition troops against the hundreds of thousands of Iraqi troops on the ground. In 100 hours of Desert Storm, the Coalition forces pushed the Iraqi army out of Kuwait and back toward the Iraqi capital, Baghdad.

Then the advance halted, and the Coalition officers signed a cease-fire with the Iraqi military. It was hailed as a great victory. Yet the aftermath of the short war spawned new controversies and raised new questions. Some asked whether the United States should have gone on to conquer all of Iraq. An opportunity to overthrow the brutal dictator Saddam Hussein seemed to have been missed. When oppressed minorities in northern and southern Iraq tried to seize their freedom in the months following the cease-fire, no Coalition forces came to their aid. American and world opinion questioned the wisdom of that decision.

In the years that followed, the United Nations maintained an embargo on trade with Iraq, promising to lift it only after international inspectors determined that Iraq no longer sought to build nuclear weapons, missiles, and chemical and biological weapons. But Iraq

Kuwaiti civilians and Coalition military forces celebrate the retreat of Iraqi forces from Kuwait. *(Defense Imagery)*

prevented those inspectors from seeing all they wanted, and again the United States and other Coalition members did not force the issue. Many outsiders suspected that Iraq secretly continued to build its high-technology new weapons.

U.S. and British aircraft patrolled "no-fly zones" in Iraq, at first to prevent the use of Iraqi aircraft against the minority rebels. But after the Iraqis quashed those rebellions, the air patrols continued for years, with intermittent exchange of missile fire between air and ground. Observers doubted whether the no-fly zones served any real purpose years after the war.

Perhaps the very success of the Persian Gulf War had fed American faith in air power and missile technology as ways of conducting a "clean" military operation that put very few Americans at risk. In any case, the United States continued its policeman role in other parts of the world. In the former Yugoslavia, ethnic rivalries among the various peoples there required peacekeeping. U.S. troops served on the ground, and then in 1998 American leaders decided to employ overwhelming air power as a tool, to force the Yugoslav government to halt its attacks on ethnic Albanians living in the province of Kosovo.

The U.S. intervention in Kosovo, part of Serbian-dominated Yugoslavia, had mixed success and mixed support among the American people. Even though the dictator of Yugoslavia, Slobodan Milosevic, was soon thrown out of office, Americans were not sure that their ideals and their self-interest had been at stake. Atrocities on both sides and ethnic hatreds continued to keep the region at the edge of war.

The lessons of the Gulf War might change how the United States plays its role as policeman and peacekeeper in the 21st century. Some believed that the Gulf War showed that air power by itself could be enough in other conflicts. Yet Iraq remained a potential threat. It might be possible for Iraq to covertly rebuild its nuclear research facilities. Perhaps Hussein's government aided terrorists in secret, a possibility that became even more alarming after the suicidal hijackings and anthrax scare of the autumn of 2001. Such issues would haunt the world in the century ahead.

Participants, scholars, and journalists have written about the war in the decade following it. The literature that they have produced divides rather clearly into several categories. First, there are the biographies, autobiographies, and memoirs of those who took part. Some of them, like *It Doesn't Take a Hero,* the autobiography of H. Norman Schwarz-kopf, give good day-to-day details of the war. Others, like Colin Powell's *My American Journey,* devote only a fairly small part of the work to the Gulf War. Even so, such books provide access to the point of view of major participants in the leadership decisions. Other works capture the memories of the soldiers in the field, like Nicholas Benson's *Rat's Tales* and Andy McNab's *Bravo Two Zero.* While vivid, such accounts are always limited by the fact that they describe only the small section of the war observed by the veterans.

At another level, a number of military and policy analysts have developed close treatments of the war. Among the best are *Desert Storm: A Forgotten War* by Alberto Bin, Richard Hill, and Archer Jones for military details; and Lawrence Freedman and Efraim Karsh's *The Gulf Conflict, 1990–1991* for diplomatic and political issues. Publication details of these and many other books and articles are provided in a further reading list at the end of this volume.

On September 11, 2001, America was shocked by the terrorist-suicide attacks on the World Trade Center and the Pentagon. Suddenly, questions about the Middle East took on a new urgency. An excellent

The U.S. Marines called their assembled unit for the liberation of Kuwait "Task Force Grizzly" and wore this shoulder patch proudly. *(Official U.S. Marine Corps Photo)*

treatment of the relationship of terrorism to recent history in the Middle East and the Persian Gulf is Yossef Bodansky's *Bin Laden: The Man Who Declared War on America.* Bodansky, a congressional staff expert on terrorism and the Middle East, first published his study in 1999, and his publishers rushed a second edition into print within a month after the 2001 attacks. Bodansky showed how one long-term consequence of U.S. defense of Saudi Arabia and Kuwait against Iraq was to fuel the antagonism of extremists such as Osama bin Laden. Bodansky provided an important perspective on the Gulf War, one that explored the long-term impact of American involvement in the Persian Gulf on America's relationship with the countries and leaders of the region.

In this revised edition of this volume in the America at War series, new color photographs and maps have been added to enhance the many illustrations throughout the text. There is a completely new chapter that discusses the weapons and tactics used and developed in the war. In addition, as in all the volumes, there is a sidebar that outlines the controversies surrounding the question of whether or not the war represents a "just war" from the American point of view. Recent literature and Web sites, published or developed since the original edition, have been added to the selection of further reading found at the end of the book.

IN THE
THICK OF IT

On August 26, 1990, Gen. Norman Schwarzkopf stepped off the airplane into an ovenlike blast of heat. It was more than 115 degrees in the shade in Saudi Arabia. Two of his senior commanders, Gen. Charles "Chuck" Horner and Gen. John Yeosock introduced him to Lieutenant General Prince Khalid bin Sultan.

Prince Khalid was the son of the minister of defense and a three-star general in the Saudi army. Schwarzkopf was a graduate of West Point, class of 1956, six foot two inches tall, and 240 pounds, known as "the Bear." Subordinates dreaded his outbursts of temper. He commanded CENTCOM, the U.S. Central Command, the paper unit that was nominally in charge of U.S. forces in a sprawling arc of 18 nations running across the troubled Middle East. One of the first steps Schwarzkopf took after issuing the order "Execute Desert Shield" was to move to Saudi Arabia. He needed to be on site to assemble the defensive forces for that country.

He set to work his headquarters staff of 700 to build up a fighting force that could stop Saddam Hussein, the Iraqi dictator, from invading Saudi Arabia. Khalid would be his liaison in a joint operation with the Saudis.

Horner and Yeosock had been struggling to make arrangements on the ground since August 7. Meanwhile, Schwarzkopf, in Tampa, Florida, where CENTCOM is headquartered, and in Washington, tried to get Joint Chiefs Chairman Colin Powell to make clear to the president and cabinet that massive forces would be needed to defend Saudi Arabia. Schwarzkopf kept insisting that an even more massive force would be needed if the decision were taken to throw Iraq out of Kuwait.

General Schwarzkopf and Lieutenant General Khalid, commander of the Joint Forces in Saudi Arabia, spell out to the Iraqis the surrender terms required on March 3, 1991, at Safwan, Iraq. (*DOD Defense Information Center, March ARB, California*)

But Horner and Yeosock ran into obstacles. Although Saudi Arabia's King Fahd had pledged them all the fuel, water, and transport they would need for incoming troops, when the Americans contacted Saudi generals, they were told, as Schwarzkopf noted in his autobiography, "We're not authorized to spend the money."

The two then appealed to Prince Sultan, minister of defense and aviation. Sultan put his son, Prince Khalid, in charge. At the air base, Khalid invited Schwarzkopf into a reception ceremony. The two officers sat together, sipping strong spiced coffee. Schwarzkopf later learned that Khalid was sizing him up, suspecting that as a four-star general who out-ranked him, Schwarzkopf would be difficult to deal with.

However, Schwarzkopf understood the culture and traditions of the Middle East in part from living as a 12-year-old in Tehran, Iran, where his father had been posted to build up the military gendarme force supporting the shah of Iran, Mohammad Reza Pahlavi. Schwarzkopf recognized that business followed after a cordial exchange of pleasantries and that knowing people personally had to come first. He and Khalid hit it off.

After the coffee ceremony, the group drove to Schwarzkopf's new offices at the Defense Ministry. Although the Saudis had provided him with a luxury suite in the Hyatt Hotel across the street, he had argued that staff should be moved out of hotels to reduce chances for terrorist attacks. Vertical targets, he warned, should be avoided. He could hardly set the example of taking up five-star quality lodgings in a high-rise after making that point.

Schwarzkopf decided to stay in the office that night, and he ended up living there for the next nine months. He had a few personal items installed: audiotapes, pictures of his family, an exercise ski machine. A secure phone line connected him directly with the chairman of the Joint Chiefs of Staff, Colin Powell, in Washington.

Five stories below ground, through heavy doors, the Saudis had converted a subbasement room into a command center, the nerve center of Desert Shield. Schwarzkopf went there immediately to get a briefing on current troop deployments.

When Schwarzkopf looked at the map of troops arranged to stop an invasion, should one occur, he was appalled. A glaring gap in the middle of the line almost invited a drive through the center. He quietly got a copy of the deployment printed out, saving it as a reminder of the sort of troop arrangements he first had encountered there, the starting point of future buildups.

He had to walk a tightrope. On the one hand, he understood that if the Iraqis attacked, thousands of lives would be lost and the Saudis and the newly arriving American troops would fight a losing battle as they pulled back. Saudi oil fields, military objectives, and cities would fall quickly before a genuine onslaught. Yet if he pressed this point too strongly with his hosts, he would alarm them.

Soon Schwarzkopf was meeting nightly with Khalid to discuss arrangements. At first they concentrated on protecting Islamic culture from the impact of the flood of Western men and women in the armed services. But Schwarzkopf tried to impress on Khalid the urgency of the situation. While this was a form of police action, it could be a military disaster.

At one midnight meeting, he pointed out that in case of attack the Defense Ministry itself could not be defended. There were guards, Schwarzkopf noted, but no bunkers. In South Vietnam, the government's ministries had put sandbags in as early as 1963, when the Communist forces started armed terror attacks in South Vietnam, targeting government facilities. Khalid was horrified. Sandbags would alarm the people. The Saudis had never done such a thing.

Hundreds of thousands of Muslim pilgrims gather annually at the shrine of the Kaaba, in the courtyard of the Great Mosque in Mecca, Saudi Arabia. Schwarzkopf worked with Khalid and others to minimize the impact of Western culture from the armed forces on the Muslims. *(Library of Congress)*

Despite his reservations, Khalid went on to take the advice. Although he avoided putting sandbags out in public, he had concrete barriers installed inside the gates and posted Saudi national guard troops in nearby streets in armored cars.

Other problems surfaced in getting Saudi customs and traditions adjusted to the realities of modern warfare. Tank commanders found that their tanks stopped working when the air filters filled with desert dust and sand. They reported the tanks disabled and waited for contract mechanics to repair them. Officers and Saudi soldiers simply did not make mechanical repairs, even to replace a filter. Some customs would have to change, as it would be hard to find civilian mechanics ready to come to the battlefront.

Schwarzkopf relied on Maj. Gen. William "Gus" Pagonis to help organize supplies and shelter for the incoming troops. Pagonis came from Pennsylvania, where his family ran a restaurant. Schwarzkopf regarded Pagonis, as he put it, as "an Einstein at making things happen." He not only rounded up equipment and supplies for the rapidly growing force, he structured his own organization out of 94 different reserve and national guard units from all over the United States. He brought together units of truck drivers, telephone installers, mechanics, and construction groups and made use of cargo handlers as more truck drivers.

Every move that Schwarzkopf made was followed closely by the international news media. He decided to take a positive attitude if he could, keeping the members of the press informed and using them to his advantage. It would be difficult. The goals of military security and public information were inherently contradictory, but with the right attitude, the modern tools of communication could serve to help, not hinder, the operation.

During the weeks that forces built up, as Schwarzkopf later noted in his memoirs, he began to feel like an athlete told to get ready for a sports event, without being told what sport he had to play. It was as if he put on a football helmet and pads, only to discover later that the game was baseball. General Powell, as chairman of the Joint Chiefs, would call on the secure telephone line one day asking for a troop rotation plan, and Schwarzkopf would have his staff develop one. A few days later, he would be told not to deliver it, because it would give the wrong political impression. Government civilians in Washington began to suggest plans, some of them unworkable, and Schwarzkopf feared that the chain of command would revert back to the pattern of the Vietnam War period, in which many felt that civilians wanted to "out-general the generals" with ideas of their own.

President George H. W. Bush and Secretary of State James Baker were working to build a coalition of forces that would assist, but the

INSTANT MEDIA

By the late 20th century, television was immediately capturing and broadcasting numerous major events: Moon landings, assassinations, and battles. The Vietnam War was the first war "fought in American living rooms," with daily film of battles, bombings, and casualties.

In 1990, some of the American public trusted television as a window on unfolding history. In Iraq and Kuwait, however, instant media created a difficult dilemma. Reporters, editors, and TV producers, and the American hunger for full disclosure expected full freedom of the media.

But to defend a broader freedom, the military felt that it had to control access to information. The Iraqis would hear and see the reports on U.S. TV and could act on the basis of news. Uncontrolled media would be like placing a weapon in the hands of an enemy, one that could be used to kill U.S. and Coalition troops and pilots. From the first arrival of troops in Saudi Arabia, the military tried to control the news flow.

diplomatic efforts went slowly. As Schwarzkopf recalled in his autobiography after returning from visiting troops in the field in late October, a staffer held out the secure phone. It was General Powell again. "The president has made a decision," said Powell. "Next weekend Secretary Baker will come to ask King Fahd and our other allies to agree to offensive operations. Then we'll take it to the U.N. and ask for an ultimatum for Iraq to leave Kuwait. You should be prepared to build up the force and go to war."

"How big a buildup do you mean?" asked Schwarzkopf.

Powell named the major units that the Pentagon agreed to send, representing nearly double the force already planned. It was a relief. But then Schwarzkopf began sweating over the issue of how to fund all the facilities and supplies that would be needed in Saudi Arabia to house the troops, estimated at some 500,000.

That evening, Schwarzkopf got another surprise. Two staffers met him with smiles. They handed him a check drawn on Morgan Guaranty Trust, with Prince Khalid's signature on it. It was for $760 million. They rushed the check by plane via Paris to New York to get it into the bank, estimating that the interest alone for a few days would yield $300,000. That could pay lots of bills.

Schwarzkopf tried to keep on good terms with the news media during the Desert Shield buildup, posing here with Katie Couric of NBC News on November 1, 1990. *(DOD Defense Information Center, March ARB, California)*

With the commitment of troops and the money, Schwarzkopf had launched into Desert Shield and later Desert Storm, which combined represented one of the most ambitious "police actions" ever taken by the United States. Some of those police actions had led into major wars, while others had been over in a day or two. This one promised to be a difficult and dangerous operation, for the challenge was massive. President Bush and his allies would have to arrange for many more millions of dollars and many more troops.

The foe was different this time as well. Saddam Hussein represented a powerful threat, and he had brazenly invaded a neighboring country. His military was strong and armed with some of the world's most threatening new weapons. He controlled vast wealth, derived from one of the richest reserves of petroleum in the world. And the politics of his move came out of the troubled history of the region.

Schwarzkopf knew the mixed record of successful and failed U.S. police actions. He also knew the enemy, and he was familiar with the Middle East, knowledge that he needed before he committed his forces to action. But the question that confronted him now was, "Would America be able to win and keep friends in this part of the world?"

THE UNITED STATES AS PEACEKEEPER AND POLICEMAN

From the earliest days of the American republic, U.S. presidents have sent the nation's armed forces overseas only for what they thought were very good reasons. The reasons were usually to stand up for American ideals such as maintaining international law or protecting small nations. At the same time, the nation also protected its political and economic interests. Some police actions took only a few days or, in some cases, only a few hours and achieved their goals almost immediately. Others that began on a small scale led into larger conflicts, some with many casualties. U.S. history had a lot to say about such risks when President George H. W. Bush and his team considered taking action in distant Kuwait.

The Atlantic and Pacific Oceans had long isolated the United States from most of the world's problems. So the U.S. Navy and the U.S. Marines, rather than the U.S. Army, fought most of the international policing actions ordered by the president in the first century of American history. The lyrics of the marine anthem recall specific expeditions with the words, "From the halls of Montezuma to the shores of Tripoli."

The modern Defense Department calls police and peacekeeping actions "Military Operations Other Than War," or MOOTWs. In MOOTWs, economic and political interests of the United States frequently meshed with idealism. The self-interest often involved protecting U.S. property or helping a friendly country. The ideals included preserving law and coming to the aid of victims of aggression or oppression.

In some MOOTWs, sailors and troops have acted like police. In other operations, U.S. servicepeople have acted more like peacekeepers, attempting to maintain peace in some troubled spot in the world where hostilities had just ended or where it seemed they might begin. Often the presence of U.S. troops could maintain law and order and help maintain a fragile peace between local forces that would go to war if the Americans and other international peacekeepers were not there. Peacekeeping and policing could be very similar in some locations.

Some of the wars in which Americans participated grew out of a MOOTW. The wars against the Barbary pirates in the years 1801 to 1805 and 1815 were probably the first wars that the United States

PIRATES, BANDITS, AND TERRORISTS

In most major American wars, the United States fought against nations that supported armies and navies, and U.S. soldiers and sailors engaged more or less equally well-equipped forces on the other side. However, the United States sometimes used its forces in actions against smaller, unorganized groups. Even though small in number, groups of pirates, bandits, and terrorists could pose a serious threat to American sailors and troops.

In the 19th century, the U.S. Navy fought against pirates in the Caribbean and in the China Sea. The navy joined with the British Royal Navy, sending the West African Squadron to suppress armed Atlantic Ocean slave traders in the 1840s and 1850s. Pancho Villa, one of the leaders of the Mexican Revolution, made raids into the United States in 1916, and the U.S. Army pursued his forces deep into Mexico, but failed make a capture.

In the late 20th century, the Defense Department termed such military attacks as "asymmetrical" warfare because the opposing forces were not equally powerful. Small groups or individuals faced the larger, regular forces on the U.S. side. One of the most difficult forms of asymmetrical warfare was the use of terror tactics by independent groups not sponsored by a particular national government.

During some American wars, the enemy would use terror or asymmetrical methods. When Iraq invaded Kuwait, American embassies and American troops stationed around the world went on high alert to guard against terrorist attacks from independent groups that might support the Iraqi position.

This copy of a work by the artist William Bainbridge-Hoff shows a naval engagement between a U.S. vessel and a ship of Barbary pirates in 1801. *(National Archives and DOD Defense Visual Information Center)*

fought as a policeman of the world. In 1801, the U.S. Navy went to the Mediterranean to stop corsairs from capturing and holding American ships and sailors for ransom. The corsairs were private ships on contract with North African princes to enforce their control of the sea. Several states along the North African coast charged foreign ships tribute, almost like a toll. Such charges violated the customary practice of European countries and the United States. Europeans and Americans regarded the high seas as open to all traffic without charge.

The American press treated the corsairs from Tripoli and neighboring countries as pirates. The American public usually supported American sailors and U.S. Marines in this early policing role. Ideals and self-interest merged in fighting for a principle and at the same time protecting American sailors and ships.

The expeditions against the Barbary corsairs were more in the nature of policing, but Americans often remembered these actions as the Barbary Wars.

The U.S. Navy went on many such expeditions, not all of them as famous or well remembered as the Barbary Wars. Some of the so-called MOOTWs were very small. In 1832, an American expedition burned Quallah Battoo, a pirate town in what is now Indonesia. The pirates there had been raiding American merchant ships that opened the

China trade from Massachusetts. The punitive, or punishing, expedition achieved its goal of stopping those particular pirates.

In the same years, the navy established regular cruises to fight piracy in the Caribbean Sea. Before the Civil War, the American West African Squadron worked with the British Royal Navy to put down the trade in slaves from West Africa to countries such as Cuba and Brazil. So, early in U.S. history, the navy had a reputation as acting in a policeman's role around the world, sometimes leading to incidents of gunfire and conflict, and even sometimes leading into a bigger war.

The U.S. military often enforced international or national law based on sound ideals. In the Barbary Wars and at Quallah Battoo, the United States fought for freedom of the seas. The United States outlawed the slave trade by treaty and U.S. law, enforced by the West African Squadron. And at the same time, all those military actions also protected American economic and political interests.

Closer to home, in 1916, a Mexican leader, Pancho Villa, led an attack into the United States in southern New Mexico. American troops under Gen. John "Blackjack" Pershing pursued Villa on a fruitless expedition far into Mexico. The U.S. Army used aircraft as well as cavalry to hunt for Villa in this "perishing expedition," as the press liked to call it. Though the Americans never caught Villa, Blackjack Pershing had used U.S. military forces to try to enforce law and to protect American interests.

The United States has had mixed reasons for entry into some major wars. Often a major war began from both self-interest and an effort to preserve a principle of law. So even major wars sometimes grew out of MOOTWs.

The Korean War in 1950 to 1953 started after North Korea invaded South Korea. The United Nations voted to protect South Korea, and U.S. forces played the largest part in this police action. The American public often wondered during the war if fighting in Korea really served the interest of the United States. But political leaders of both major parties made it clear that world peace would best be preserved if the United States and its allies stood firm against such an act of aggression. The American public and U.S. troops grew resentful that diplomats and politicians called the war that killed some 33,000 Americans a "police action."

In more recent times, the United States frequently sent troops overseas, often with the same goals of preserving order, stopping criminals,

During a 1983 operation in Grenada, U.S. Marines took up patrol duties after the takeover. *(DOD Defense Information Center, March ARB, California)*

and protecting American interests. President Ronald Reagan intended that the U.S. invasion of the island of Grenada in 1983 stop the takeover of the island by a government friendly to Cuban leader Fidel Castro. The claims that American students there were in danger helped some Americans see the invasion as a case of protecting law and order. Critics of the Grenada invasion believed the real reason was to challenge the spread of communism and that the students were in no danger.

In 1989, U.S. troops in Operation Just Cause invaded Panama to arrest the president of that country, Manuel Noriega. Noriega had become wealthy and powerful through his control of the trade in illegal drugs. Again, Americans fought the short war for the purpose of protecting law and order and at the same time to protect U.S. interests.

Americans have often debated whether they fought a particular war for genuine idealistic reasons. Critics often claimed that some private economic interest really led to the military action. They have charged that the ideals served just as window dressing in some instances. When the American public believed that their people died for private gain rather than public good, they became very disillusioned about the use of military power.

After World War I many Americans felt that the country had gone into that war for ideals that were not genuine. Many thought that their troops fought simply to enrich weapons makers and other industrialists. U.S. president Woodrow Wilson had hoped to establish a lasting peace by getting countries to agree to join the League of Nations. But in the United States, a period of isolationism followed World War I. The country stayed out of the League of Nations, partly because of this disillusionment in Wilson's ideals.

A similar disillusionment in the stated ideals of the Vietnam War led to the so-called Vietnam syndrome after the U.S. withdrawal in 1974 to 1975. That term referred to the idea that Americans were not willing to support a war overseas without a clear understanding and support for the war's goals.

In December 1989, U.S. Marines invaded Panama to arrest Gen. Manuel Noriega on drug charges. Here a U.S. soldier talks on a field telephone; on the wall behind him is a T-shirt supporting Noriega, presumably a type worn by Panamanians before the invasion. *(Defense Imagery)*

In every case when U.S. ships and troops went overseas to fight, they went to a "hot spot." The hot spots were always places where the U.S. government believed or at least argued that local leaders were violating the law. Sometimes it was domestic, or national, law of the country, and often it was a case of an international law or practice that was violated. Usually the violation of law affected American business and economic interests, but not always. A wide variety of different reasons could turn a local conflict into a U.S. concern.

When fighting corsairs and pirates, the United States sent the navy and marines to protect American shipping and American businesses. However, the major countries of the world outlawed piracy, and the United States was enforcing international law while it protected American ships. In such cases, ideals and self-interest meshed perfectly.

At times a major foreign navy would attack U.S. ships. French ships attacked American ships, setting off the Quasi-War, or Naval War with France, in 1799. British ships seized American ships, setting off the War of 1812. Either an accident or a terrorist act destroyed the American battleship *Maine* in Havana Harbor, starting the Spanish-American War in 1898. German submarines attacked U.S. merchant ships in 1917, bringing the United States into World War I. These hot spots at sea all arose around either U.S. merchant ships or U.S. naval ships and the right to travel from port to port around the world.

But sometimes a hot spot had nothing to do with ships and was located on dry land. When Pancho Villa raided New Mexico, he came on horseback and was pursued by people on horseback, in armored cars, and in airplanes. In 1950, when North Korea invaded South Korea, the attack was led by tanks and troops on foot and in trucks. When the United States sent troops to Grenada in 1983, it was the local government that created a hot spot. When the United States went into Panama in 1989, it was because a criminal who headed the country could not be stopped any other way.

When Gen. Norman Schwarzkopf led a coalition of U.S. and international troops against Iraq in 1990, he went on orders from President George H. W. Bush and under the authority of United Nations resolutions to prevent the Iraqi army from invading across the border into Saudi Arabia. The Iraqis had seized Kuwait in a brutal and unprovoked attack, and the U.S. government and other friendly governments feared the Iraqis would move into Saudi Arabia.

This cartoon from 1916 refers to the Mexican rebel general Pancho Villa's having crossed the border and raided a town in the United States. Uncle Sam says, "I've had about enough of this," and jumps the fence in pursuit. *(National Archives)*

Once again, American ideals and self-interest were both involved. Iraqi president Saddam Hussein had ordered his troops to take over Kuwait. It was the first time that one member nation of the United Nations had made an uninvited invasion and conquered a neighboring nation that was also a member of the United Nations. Hussein had simply violated a very basic principle of international law and the principle of national sovereignty.

But the Kuwait–Saudi Arabia border was also a hot spot for financial reasons. Kuwait had more than 90 billion barrels of crude oil reserves in the ground, nearly as much as Iraq. Saudi Arabia and the smaller Persian Gulf countries accounted for more than 40 percent of the world's supply of oil. If Hussein's army seized those nations, it would be almost impossible to get him out, and he would be able to control more than half the world supply of oil, including that in Iraq and Kuwait.

Americans could clearly see that ideals and self-interest came together in this new hot spot. Although the Gulf War would be like many others in American history, springing from ideals and self-interest, it had many distinctive aspects.

Americans were surprised to learn that Hussein's army was the fourth largest in the world (after those of China, Russia, and Vietnam). The U.S. Army was only the seventh largest. Americans were also surprised to learn that Iraq had a huge supply of poison gas—and might be ready to build nuclear weapons.

General Schwarzkopf, President Bush, and other American leaders had to know how such a threat had developed. They tried to understand whether Hussein's claim to Kuwait had any basis in international law. Schwarzkopf had to understand exactly how powerful the Iraqi forces were and whether the U.S. and allied troops rushing to Saudi Arabia were strong enough to stop Hussein.

President Bush and General Schwarzkopf also had to gauge American popular reactions. Recent history suggested that the Vietnam syndrome would set in, and the U.S. public would grow cynical about the reasons and suspect that oil politics, not protection of sovereignty, led them to war.

Other issues required sensitivity. The Arabian people, as devout and strict Muslims, probably would not welcome a flood of soldiers from non-Muslim countries. Some of the Saudi leaders were more afraid that the foreign soldiers would undermine their culture than they were afraid of an attack from Hussein's army.

U.S. troops who flew to Saudi Arabia were like Americans who for nearly 200 years served in peacekeeping and policing. But in 1990, they faced a very different situation, one with its own unique background.

THE MIDDLE EAST SITUATION

The "Middle East" is a term that the British devised to refer to the area to the south and east of Europe, closer than the "Far East." Because the term is so vague, it sometimes refers to a whole group of mostly Arab-speaking nations stretching from Morocco on the northwest tip of Africa, across North Africa, through Turkey, Syria, Israel, Lebanon, Jordan, Iraq, Iran, Afghanistan, Kuwait, and the countries on the Arabian Peninsula. Sometimes newspapers use the term Middle East to refer only to Israel and its neighbors: Lebanon, Syria, Jordan, Egypt, and the territory under the control of the Palestinian Authority.

Although Arabic is spoken throughout the region, some peoples in the region speak other languages: Turkish in Turkey; Hebrew and English in Israel; Farsi in Iran; Kurdish in the mountains where Iraq, Syria, and Turkey meet; and Pashtun and other languages in Afghanistan. Arabs speaking one or another dialect of the Arabian language feel a common bond of brotherhood.

Still another bond comes from the fact that the majority of people throughout the Middle East share the religion of Islam. Most of the population of Egypt, Syria, Jordan, Iraq, and Saudi Arabia are Arabic-speaking Muslims. Yet history, geography, politics, money, and religion have sorely divided even these nations.

The troubles in this hot spot of the world have their roots in earlier history. At the beginning of the 20th century, the weak and divided Ottoman Empire, controlled out of Turkey, stretched from the edge of southeastern Europe bordering Greece, down the eastern side of the Mediterranean, and down both coasts of the Arabian Peninsula. During World War I, the Ottoman Empire sided with Germany and Austria-Hungary against the Allied powers: England,

France, Russia, and later, the United States. In the interior of the Arabian Peninsula, the Arabs fought, with British help, against the Ottoman Empire.

At the end of World War I, the peace conference at Versailles in France redrew the maps of Europe and the Middle East. Led by the United States, England, France, and Italy, the conference decided to divide up both the Austro-Hungarian Empire and the Ottoman Empire into smaller nations. In Europe, the former countries of the Austro-Hungarian Empire were made independent and self-governing, more or less along ethnic lines. Although the United States did not join, the new League of Nations continued the work of the Versailles Conference. The core of the Ottoman Empire emerged as the self-

The mosque of Sultan Suleiman is located in Istanbul (formerly Constantinople), the political capital of the Ottoman Empire, in what is today Turkey. *(Library of Congress)*

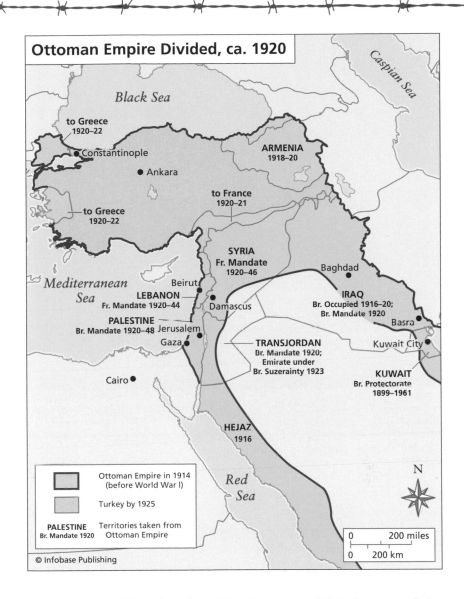

Ottoman Empire Divided, ca. 1920

Black Sea

to Greece
1920–22

Constantinople

Ankara

ARMENIA
1918–20

to France
1920–21

to Greece
1920–22

SYRIA
Fr. Mandate
1920–46

Baghdad

Mediterranean
Sea

Beirut

LEBANON
Fr. Mandate 1920–44

Damascus

IRAQ
Br. Occupied 1916–20;
Br. Mandate 1920

PALESTINE
Br. Mandate 1920–48

Jerusalem

Gaza

TRANSJORDAN
Br. Mandate 1920;
Emirate under
Br. Suzerainty 1923

Basra

Kuwait City

Cairo

KUWAIT
Br. Protectorate
1899–1961

HEJAZ
1916

Caspian Sea

Ottoman Empire in 1914
(before World War I)

Turkey by 1925

PALESTINE
Br. Mandate 1920

Territories taken from
Ottoman Empire

Red
Sea

N

0   200 miles

0   200 km

© Infobase Publishing

governing republic of Turkey. The league established some of the
Arab countries to the south and east of Turkey as "mandates." This
meant that a European country administered the region, almost like a
colony. Eventually, the Europeans were to turn over control to a local
self-governing regime. France controlled Lebanon and Syria, with the
British occupying and administering Palestine, Iraq, and Kuwait. The
British also "protected" the Persian Gulf countries of Qatar, Bahrain
(an island), and a group of states headed by emirs, later organized as
the United Arab Emirates.

A massive crowd assembles to witness the signing of the Treaty of Versailles, June 28, 1919. *(National Archives)*

For the large territory of the Arabian Peninsula, the British and other major world powers accepted the regime of King Ibn Saud as an independent nation, partly because the Saudi Arabians had fought against the Ottoman Turks on the side of the Allies during World War I. By 1926, Ibn Saud united two former Ottoman provinces, Nejd and Hejaz. By 1932, Saud reigned over the country as the United Kingdom of Saudi Arabia. In the 1990s, King Fahd, a son of Ibn Saud, ruled.

In some of the other countries that had been carved out of the Ottoman Empire, however, Britain and France appeared to the Arab people to be reluctant to convert their mandates into independent nations. Britain recognized the independence of Iraq as a monarchy in 1932. But France granted Lebanon full self-government only in 1944, and Syria did not achieve independence until 1946. Britain held the mandate for Palestine, but after World War II, Jewish settlers in Palestine fought for their independence from Britain; by 1948 the state of Israel was recognized as controlling most of Palestine. However, Britain continued to administer the province of Kuwait until 1961 and did not withdraw its protectorate status over the smaller emirates and sheik-doms of the Persian Gulf until 1971.

With such policies, the Europeans and later the Americans sowed seeds of long-term resentment by the Arab peoples and their local rulers against the Europeans. Britain, for instance, had divided some of the lands of the Ottoman Empire with new boundaries. The Ottoman Empire had included Kuwait in the province of Basra, well inside the borders of modern Iraq, and Iraqis still claimed that the British division that made Kuwait a separate country was not only arbitrary but illegitimate. Other nations did not recognize Iraq's claim, but the issue would come back to serve Saddam Hussein as a kind of legal basis for his decision to invade Kuwait. The later rulers and most of the people of Kuwait, however, were satisfied with the British lines of demarcation that set Kuwait as a separate mandate from that of Iraq and later allowed its establishment as an independent nation.

The United States recognized the importance of Saudi Arabia as an oil-producing region during the 1940s. Here, U.S. president Franklin D. Roosevelt meets with Saudi king Ibn Saud in Egypt. *(Franklin D. Roosevelt Presidential Library)*

The region became important in world trade in the 1930s. Crude oil reserves in Iraq and Kuwait and and new discoveries along the coast of the Persian Gulf in Bahrain and in Saudi Arabia, began to bring in vast amounts of money. As the world consumption of petroleum products, particularly gasoline, climbed rapidly through the years 1919–39, between World War I and World War II, the world's future supply of oil became crucial. European and American oil companies began to work closely with the independent Saudis and Iraqis, and with the emirs and sheiks whose regions were under British protection. In a number of agreements, U.S. oil companies such as Standard Oil and Texaco worked with British Petroleum and the Dutch/British company Shell Oil to share among themselves the rich oil fields found in the region.

The amount of crude oil under the surface of the land has always been difficult to determine. But as oil workers discovered more reserves, the question of the political leaning and friendliness of each local ruler to the oil companies became more and more important. During and immediately after World War II, most of the local governments willingly accepted an arrangement in which the oil companies

TANKERS AND OIL RIGS

The Middle East holds the world's largest known reserves of oil, and it transports most of this oil overseas. The oil is reached by drilling a well down to the oil-bearing sand. A tall oil rig over the well holds the drill. Workers use the rig to connect lengths of pipe to drill deeper. Underground pressure or pumps drive the crude oil to the surface. Some oil companies pipe the crude to local refineries where they break it down into gasoline, diesel fuel, heating oil, lubricants, and asphalt. However, most of the crude oil is piped overland to a seaport, then pumped into large oceangoing tanker ships destined for refineries in Japan, Europe, or the United States.

Since crude oil is inflammable, rigs, pipelines, and tankers are extremely vulnerable to attack. During the 1980s war between Iraq and Iran, the Iranians tried to cut off Iraq's source of money by sinking tankers carrying Iraqi crude. In the Gulf War, the retreating Iraqis set fire to scores of oil wells and opened pipes into the Persian Gulf, creating a major environmental disaster.

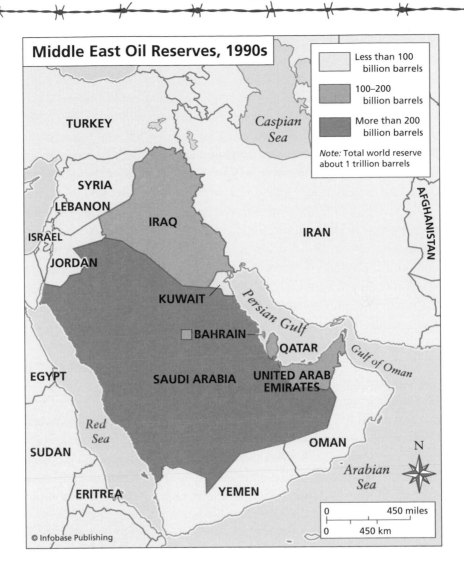

Middle East Oil Reserves, 1990s

Less than 100 billion barrels

100–200 billion barrels

More than 200 billion barrels

Note: Total world reserve about 1 trillion barrels

TURKEY

Caspian Sea

SYRIA

LEBANON

IRAQ

IRAN

ISRAEL

AFGHANISTAN

JORDAN

KUWAIT

Persian Gulf

BAHRAIN

QATAR

Gulf of Oman

EGYPT

SAUDI ARABIA

UNITED ARAB EMIRATES

Red Sea

OMAN

N

SUDAN

Arabian Sea

ERITREA

YEMEN

0   450 miles

0   450 km

© Infobase Publishing

would pay a tax to the local regime for every barrel of crude oil pumped from the ground.

However, beginning in the 1960s and 1970s, the oil-producing countries changed all that. The local governments made it clear that the oil belonged to them, and they permitted the oil companies only to operate the wells, pipelines, and the shipping facilities. This meant that in each of these Arab countries, a government official regulated the quantity of oil pumped and sold. The producing countries allowed the oil companies only operating costs and a fraction of the profits, retaining the bulk of the earnings as revenue to the government, whether ruled by a sheik, king, emir, or president. In particular, Iraq, Kuwait, and Saudi Arabia began to earn enormous revenues, representing billions of dollars per year.

By the 1970s, many of the countries producing crude oil joined the Organization of Petroleum Exporting Countries (OPEC). This organization, founded in 1960, included in 1990 13 nations from South America, Africa, the Middle East, and Southeast Asia that depended heavily on oil exports for their national income. Because these nations' combined production represented such a large percentage of the world's output, OPEC was able to control the world price of oil. Each country's oil minister could limit production according to an OPEC agreement. Often, however, one or more of the countries, after agreeing to limit production to create a shortage and drive up prices, would allow more production. OPEC could not enforce the agreement on the member countries, and some individual countries cheated on the agreement to get more money.

Although different experts make different estimates, there are some basic figures about the amount of oil reserves in Iraq, Kuwait, Saudi Arabia, and the Gulf States (Bahrain, Qatar, and the United Arab Emirates). Crude oil is measured in barrels, even though some of it is directly piped from wells to tankers and then shipped across the ocean to be piped into huge tanks and refineries, never seeing the inside of a real barrel. A crude oil barrel as a unit of measurement is 42 U.S. gallons. At the end of the 20th century, these figures showed that together Iraq, Kuwait, and the countries of the Arabian Peninsula had more than half of the world's petroleum reserves.

Although Kuwait had the smallest of these reserves, it had a small population, so Kuwaitis soon grew wealthy. The government provided free college education and health care to its citizens. "Guest workers" from poorer countries, such as India and Pakistan, performed most of the hard labor. Next door, Iraq had larger oil reserves, but it was far more populous and still held vast pockets of poverty. So the great oil wealth, even in the days after OPEC, only sharpened some of the differences among Arabs and Muslims.

Territorial disputes between peoples in the Middle East, as elsewhere in the world, have also led to many conflicts. The conflict between the Jewish state of Israel and the largely Muslim population of Palestine and the Arab countries bordering Israel and Palestine has produced four major wars and many clashes since Israel's independence in 1948.

WORLDWIDE OIL RESERVES

Total world reserves	about 1,000 billion barrels
Saudi reserves	about 260 billion barrels
Gulf States reserves	about 105 billion barrels
Iraqi reserves	about 100 billion barrels
Kuwaiti reserves	about 95 billion barrels

Realizing a dream of many European Jews to restore a homeland in the Near East, individual Jews emigrated from Europe in the late 19th century and early 20th century to settle in Palestine, at first within the Ottoman Empire, later as a British mandate. Immediately following World War II, in the period 1945–48, thousands of surviving Jews in Europe demanded access to the settlements in Palestine. The British held back the flood of immigrants as best they could, knowing that the Muslim population of Palestine resented the Jewish settlers. In 1947, the United Nations resolved to partition Palestine into a Jewish state and an Arab state. Finally, on May 14, 1948, Israel declared its independence and the British withdrew.

Following World War II, thousands of Jewish refugees from Europe fled to Palestine, where the state of Israel was established in 1948. These three young people had been liberated from the concentration camp at Buchenwald in 1945. *(National Archives)*

Immediately, the surrounding Arabic states declared war on Israel. Israel won these battles, signing separate armistice agreements with its neighbors in 1949. Egypt controlled one Arab zone of Palestine, the Gaza Strip near its border, while Jordan controlled the West Bank, a section of Palestine to the west of the Jordan River. Neither country granted independence to the Palestinians under their control.

In a series of three more wars in 1956, 1967, and 1973, Israel was able to defeat its Arab neighbors. Israel occupied and administered the two Arab regions of Palestine, making Gaza and the West Bank the occupied territories. Under negotiated settlements, Israel withdrew from the territories, and a self-governing Palestinian Authority administered the Gaza Strip and West Bank regions. The struggle of Palestinian Arabs to convert those territories into a self-governing state continued as a source of conflict in that corner of the Middle East, as Israeli settlers established housing and communities inside both the Gaza Strip and West Bank. Arabs and Muslims around the world tended to see the continued Israeli settlements and military actions in Gaza and the West Bank as the oppression of their people. When the United States provided financial and diplomatic help to Israel, it appeared to many that the United States shared in the oppression of legitimate national aspirations. So the Israel-Palestine issue, along with all the other troubles of the Middle East, represented part of the background facing the United States when Hussein invaded Kuwait.

Less familiar to Americans than the Israel-Palestine issue is the division between two different types of Muslims in that part of the world. The Arabs of Saudi Arabia, Kuwait, and the minority population of Iraq are Sunni Muslims, while the non-Arab, Farsi-speaking Persians of Iran are mostly Shiite Muslims. The majority of Iraqis are also Shiite. The leaders of Syria belong to one sect of Shiites, as do some Muslims in the small country of Bahrain. The differences between Sunni and Shiite Muslims have to do with religious doctrine and with differing beliefs about the successors to the original Muslim prophet, Muhammad. Also, among the Shiites, holy men tend to have far more nonreligious authority than among Sunni Muslims. A strict Shiite regime took over Farsi-speaking Iran from the pro-American shah there in 1979.

The difference between Sunni and Shiite regimes contributed to the bitter war from 1980 to 1988 between Iraq and Iran, along with disputes over the exact border between the two countries. When Iraq went to war with Iran in September 1980, the United States stayed officially neutral. The U.S. government, however, favored the Iraqi government under Saddam Hussein during the war.

The United States demonstrated the favoritism in several ways. The U.S. government cut off arms sales to Iran but placed no such embargo on Iraq. When Israeli aircraft bombed an Iraqi nuclear research reactor at Osiraq, outside Baghdad, in 1981, the United States joined in supporting a United Nations resolution condemning the action of Israel. By 1984, the United States and Iraq had established diplomatic relations and exchanged ambassadors. The United States even provided information to Iraq about Iranian troop movements beginning in 1986. In 1989 the United States sold more than $1 billion in goods to Iraq, including high-tech computers.

In 1979 Iranian army demonstrators supported the fundamentalist cleric Ayatollah Khomeini and expressed their hostility to the United States. *(Hulton Archive/Getty Images)*

In the light of later developments, the U.S. support for the Iraqi regime of Saddam Hussein seemed to have been a mistaken policy. However, Democratic president Jimmy Carter and Republican presidents Ronald Reagan and George H. W. Bush (in the first months he held office) tended to favor Iraq. So did members of both American political parties in Congress. Iraq's government fought against the extreme fundamentalists of Iran who had been so anti-American. That alone seemed to convince many in the United States that the pro-Iraq stand was a good idea.

In March 1988, Saddam Hussein's forces used poison gas to kill thousands of Kurdish civilians and Iranian troops in the Iraqi town of Halabja. Even so, American farmers and lobbyists for business supported the U.S. administration when it refused to issue sanctions against Iraq, such as limiting exports. When idealism about the rights of minorities came in conflict with self-interest in the form of good business and shared anti-Iranian politics, idealism lost out.

During its war with Iran, Iraq relied on oil revenue—so-called petrodollars—to pay for weapons, so Iranian ships and aircraft attacked tankers in the Persian Gulf that carried Iraqi oil, hoping to cut off this source of funds. The oil tanker companies had registered some of the ships carrying the oil in Kuwait, and the United States agreed to allow the ships to reregister under the American flag. In this way, the United States even provided the protection of the U.S. flag to help Iraq.

By 1990, Iraq had become a powerful country, despite its long and inconclusive war with neighboring Iran. Part of the reason Iraq was able to threaten and intimidate neighboring countries was because of its large well-trained army. Although estimates varied, the Western press often claimed that Hussein's army numbered 1 million. Another reason was that the country had spent billions of its oil revenue on a number of very sophisticated new weapons.

When Saddam Hussein threatened the small country of Kuwait and demanded financial compensation from Kuwait and Saudi Arabia to help pay outstanding bills in 1990, he supplemented his military forces with new weapons of mass destruction. When Kuwait and Saudi Arabia offered some funds, Hussein demanded more. The new weapons that he used to back up his demands included poison gas and ballistic missiles, reputedly with enough range to reach far into Saudi Arabia and even across Jordan into Israel. Furthermore, the media reported

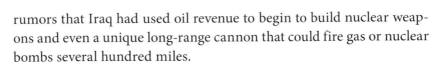

rumors that Iraq had used oil revenue to begin to build nuclear weapons and even a unique long-range cannon that could fire gas or nuclear bombs several hundred miles.

Suddenly, a country that had seemed almost like a friend to the United States in the troubled region appeared ready to upset the balance.

HUSSEIN AND MODERN WEAPONS

After a series of military governments that replaced the Iraqi monarchy in 1958, Saddam Hussein emerged in 1979 as the head of state and head of government. Soon after taking full power, he launched his war against Iran in 1980 while continuing to rule his own country with an iron hand. He used as a major instrument of power his control of the Baath Party.

In Arabic, *bath* is the word for "renaissance" or "rebirth." The party, originally formed in Syria in the 1940s, stood for Arab unity or pan-Arabism, trying to bridge the gaps between Muslim and non-Muslim Arabs and between Sunni and Shiite Muslims. Borrowing ideas from both communism and fascism, the party offered a vision of the future based on racial identity.

Hussein had attracted support from other Baathist military men for his daring role in a failed assassination attempt against a rival military leader in 1959. Escaping with his life, disguised as a desert Bedouin tribesman, he made his way to Syria and then to Egypt, where he enrolled in law school.

When the Baath Party succeeded in taking power in Iraq in 1963, Saddam Hussein went home to establish a set of security and intelligence agencies for the new government. Using that base and his family connections, he soon emerged as a strongman behind the nominal ruler as early as 1968. One of his first acts after taking full power in 1979 was to order the execution of 21 former cabinet members, including one of his closest associates. Although verifiable facts are scarce, according to legend, he had each one personally shot by 29 machine guns wielded by party officials. Some of the victims had as many as 500 bullet wounds.

Baathism under Saddam Hussein provided a tool to try to unite his diverse country. The country had a largely Sunni population but had a large Shiite minority in the southern region bordering Iran. Although Sunni, the Kurdish population in the northwest of the nation sought independence. Elsewhere, fierce local loyalties to family, clan, and tribe worked to prevent unity.

The Kurds represent about 20 percent of Iraq's population, and their desire for an independent homeland especially challenged Hussein's plans for national unity. In 1974, Hussein ordered two Kurdish towns of more than 20,000 inhabitants leveled. Attacking pilots regularly used napalm, or jellied gasoline, to burn out the Kurdish civilians. The *Times* of London estimated that the attacks on the Kurds in the early 1970s uprooted 1.5 million people and made them into refugees. Iraqi troops forced more than 100,000 Kurds from Iraq into Iran. Iraqi soldiers simply gunned down Kurdish resistance fighters who tried to surrender and lay down their arms. The Iraqi government forcibly resettled a large number of Kurds from their mountain homelands in the desert of southwestern Iraq. Although the government kept the total number secret, estimates ranged from 50,000 to 350,000 in this resettlement.

Saddam Hussein used all the modern tools of propaganda and military force before and after the Iraqi invasion of Kuwait to maintain his regime in power. *(Hulton/Archive)*

Kurdish women prepare a meal outside their home during the period after the end of Operation Desert Storm, when the United Nations enforced a no-fly zone over Kurdish territory to prevent Iraqi forces from attacking the Kurds. *(Defense Imagery)*

Hussein was not only brutal with the Kurds but he also developed a reputation for brutality and ruthless control over his own forces. According to one story, when a cabinet minister suggested that he should temporarily step down during the Iranian war, Hussein took the official into another room and there shot the man to death himself. Rumors told of a similar story about a general who warned that a planned attack during the Iranian war would result in high casualties. Whether or not Hussein actually killed either the cabinet minister or the general, many Iraqis believed the stories, contributing to the fear and respect shown him by his subordinates.

In 1982, a reporter from the German magazine *Stern* interviewed Hussein about rumors of ruthless executions.

"It is known that your Excellency is not satisfied with the Iraqi military command," said the reporter. "Is it true that in the recent period, 300 high ranking military officers have been executed?"

"No," said Hussein. "However, two divisional commanders and the commanders of a mechanized unit were executed." He paused and looked at the reporter. He went on, "This is something very normal in all wars."

The reporter from *Stern* asked, "For what reason?"

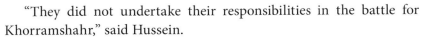

"They did not undertake their responsibilities in the battle for Khorramshahr," said Hussein.

Many other shocking stories came out of Iraq. For example, one former senior official of the Baath Party was present at a social gathering in 1987 when several people made jokes about Saddam Hussein. The government later arrested him for not informing on the others present. Security forces tortured him and his family members, executed him and his family, and later bulldozed their home to the ground. Public insult of the president or the ruling party remains punishable by life imprisonment or death in Iraq. Frequently when an individual who was accused could not be located, a member of his family was rounded up, tortured, and then executed. After the execution, the police would deliver the body back to the family and present them with a bill for the coffin.

Even though Hussein governed through ruthless control and fear, the country prospered. The nation modernized, and the Baath Party could take credit for improving education, raising the status of women, and bringing clean drinking water and electricity to remote villages. Hussein himself lived in an assortment of palaces and generally wore a bulletproof vest during his working days. Soon workers plastered public walls throughout Iraq with huge murals and photos of Saddam Hussein. He remained devoted to his family, and whether through fear, admiration, or both, the Iraqi people constantly praised him. Like other dictators before him in Germany, Italy, the Soviet Union, and elsewhere in the world, a cult of personality grew around Hussein that made his control even stronger.

During the war with Iran, Iraq spent more than $80 billion on weapons. In 1984 alone, the country spent more than $33 billion, an amount representing about 30 percent of the country's total budget. In 1989 Iraq spent some $15 billion. Most of the weapons came from France, China, and the Soviet Union. Even though Britain imposed an embargo on arms sales to Iraqi, British companies sold many defense-related goods to the country. Computerized equipment from Britain and the United States helped Hussein build up his local arms industry. It was rumored that the British sold so many desert uniforms to the Iraqis that when their soldiers went to fight against Hussein in 1991, Britain had no desert uniforms left to equip their own troops.

The Soviet Union sold SS-1 missiles to Iraq. Known as "Scuds," these surface-to-surface missiles had a range of about 190 miles. The Iraqis modified the missiles, sometimes by welding two together, and increased their range to a reputed 560 miles. Iraqi technicians had to reduce the delivered explosive, or payload, and the Scuds remained very inaccurate. They could not be guaranteed to land within a mile of a specified target at such a long range. The U.S. Central Intelligence Agency (CIA) claimed that Iraq continued to buy spares from North Korea even after the invasion of Kuwait.

But conventional hardware was only part of Hussein's arsenal. Using German and American technology, Hussein developed factories for the production of poisonous gas and weapons to deliver the gas. Iraq's nuclear weapons program moved ahead also. Using information made public in the United States, Iraqi scientists and technicians built machinery for the separation of uranium-235 that they could use in nuclear warheads. Israeli aircraft bombed the Osiraq reactor in 1981, in hopes of preventing the development of a nuclear weapon by Iraq, fearing that such a weapon could be used against Israel in an Arab-Israeli war. The Osiraq raid temporarily delayed work on the Iraqi atomic weapon. However, the program was well under way again by the late 1980s. Outside observers believed in 1990 that the Iraqis might already have made several nuclear bombs.

Both nuclear weapons and poison gas weapons are known as weapons of mass destruction, or WMDs. Hussein's forces had an unknown

The Soviet SS-1 missile, known as the Scud, was moved aboard a transporter-erector-launcher vehicle, making it hard to track down and destroy. *(DOD Defense Information Center, March ARB, California)*

Hussein's forces were equipped with improved 155 mm howitzers, similar to this U.S. model. *(DOD Defense Information Center, March ARB, California)*

quantity of WMDs that might be used. The fact that Hussein had ordered poison gas attacks on Kurds and Iranians during the war with Iran made such a threat seem more than a bluff.

Many of the weapons that the Iraqis possessed were so-called conventional weapons, but, nevertheless, Iraqis had them in impressive numbers and power. For example, the Iraqis had 300 howitzers, firing 155 mm shells. They were of an advanced design, worked out by one of the world's most sophisticated weapons engineers, Gerald Bull. One hundred of the Bull-designed howitzers carne from a South African company and had a range of 25 miles. Trucks could tow the guns to battle at 55 miles an hour, and soldiers could set them up in just a few minutes to fire between two and three shells a minute. Another 200 howitzers of the Bull design came from an Austrian company.

The Iraqis had another advanced conventional weapon in armored, self-propelled artillery pieces. Constructed in Iraq, these weapons, mounted on a six-wheeled armored vehicle, could travel 55 miles an hour on a paved road and could fire a heavy shell with a range of 23 miles. Some of these mobile guns had a reported range of 34 miles. Altogether, the Iraqis had 3,110 artillery pieces, 4,280 tanks, and 2,870 armored personnel carriers.

Even after Iraq accepted a UN resolution in August 1988, calling for an end to the long war with Iran, the Iraqi army remained strong. Saddam Hussein was able to put an army of more than 500,000 troops into

GERALD BULL AND THE SUPERGUN

Gerald Bull, a Canadian-born gun designer, had a dream of developing a gun capable of firing a satellite into orbit around the Earth. He argued that a gun, unlike a rocket, can be reused and it would be cheaper. Such a gun could allow less wealthy countries, such as Canada, to enter the exclusive club of nations with space programs. Some scientists scoffed at his ideas, but he won respect for his designs.

In 1976, Gerald Bull sold designs for improved 155 mm howitzers, with extended ranges over 20 miles, to the Republic of South Africa. The United States charged Bull with the crime of violating the U.S. embargo of South Africa. Bull offered evidence that the U.S. government had approved and even encouraged his sales. Nevertheless, he spent several months in prison for dealing with the outlawed South African regime.

In 1981, Bull moved his office to Brussels, Belgium, where he continued his arms design work. Someone methodically shot him to death there on March 22, 1990, but Belgian police never identified his killer. At the time of his death, he had arranged for the sale of three Superguns to Iraq, which when completed would have a range of several hundred miles, far greater than the improved howitzers. Several European countries were making the parts for the Superguns. Through 1990, journalists' accounts forced police to confiscate some of the equipment.

UN weapons inspectors in Iraq later found one of the guns partially constructed on a hillside and a cache of stockpiled parts for two more. Some experts argued that Iraq had intended the guns as satellite launchers. Perhaps Hussein sought the prestige of joining the small number of advanced countries that could put satellites in orbit. But as weapons, the guns could have fired poison gas or nuclear shells as far as Israel, Syria, and deep into Saudi Arabia.

the field against any who would try to defend Saudi Arabia or liberate Kuwait. Armed with its sophisticated weapons, the huge Iraqi military force was a formidable foe.

But after all the expenditures for new weapons and the many expenses of the eight-year war with Iran, the Iraqi treasury was in need of cash. While oil revenue was the strength of Iraq, it was also its weakness. When OPEC allowed oil prices to drop in 1989–90, Iraq found it

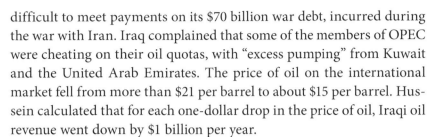

difficult to meet payments on its $70 billion war debt, incurred during the war with Iran. Iraq complained that some of the members of OPEC were cheating on their oil quotas, with "excess pumping" from Kuwait and the United Arab Emirates. The price of oil on the international market fell from more than $21 per barrel to about $15 per barrel. Hussein calculated that for each one-dollar drop in the price of oil, Iraqi oil revenue went down by $1 billion per year.

Furthermore, Hussein had other special grievances against Kuwait. During the war between Iraq and Iran, he claimed, Kuwait moved the border in the desert between the two countries about 2.5 miles and then tapped into the rich Rumaila oil field. He claimed that Kuwait had "stolen" more than $2.4 billion in oil from the field. He also alleged that slant-drilling of oil wells, in which the oil rig drives the well at an angle, allowed Kuwaitis to further draw oil from the Iraqi side of the boundary. Furthermore, much of the war debt that Iraq owed was to Kuwait, at least $10 billion. Hussein demanded that Kuwait forgive or write off the loan, on the grounds that he had been fighting in common cause with other Sunni Arabs against the Farsi-speaking Shiite Iranians.

Iraq had only 18 miles of shoreline on the Persian Gulf, much of which was blocked by Kuwait's uninhabited Bubiyan Island, largely a mudflat. The Iraqis had offered to lease the island, but Kuwait had refused, apparently in the belief that if Iraqis moved in, they would never return the territory. Finally, Saddam Hussein also used the long-standing grievance about the sovereign status of Kuwait. He brought up again the charge that when Britain gave independence to Kuwait in 1961, it had no right to do so: the territory should have remained part of Iraq, as it had been part of the Iraqi Basra province in the old Ottoman Empire. But Kuwait insisted that its separate independence was recognized under the British protectorate and that it had long received international recognition as an independent nation.

In July 1900, Hussein moved 30,000 troops to the Kuwaiti border and then, at a meeting of OPEC, he forced Kuwait and the United Arab Emirates to agree to abide by their oil-producing quota and to work for a higher price of oil. Despite this victory on the oil question, Hussein then moved additional troops to the border. Observers in Europe, the United States, and Kuwait thought Hussein may have intended to intimidate Kuwait into concessions on the Bubiyan Island question.

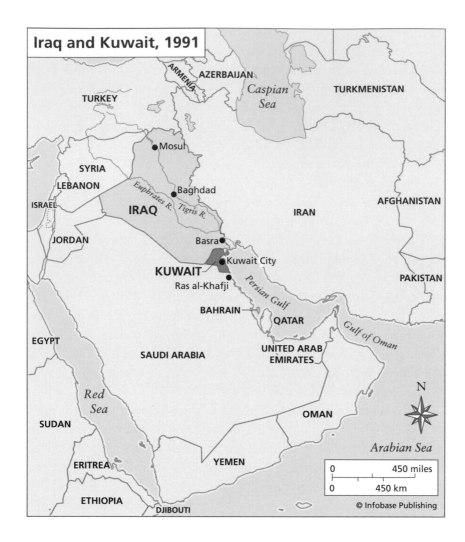

Iraq and Kuwait, 1991

But whether a bluff or a preparation for an invasion, the threat seemed powerful.

The U.S. ambassador to Iraq was April Glaspie. On July 25, 1990, Hussein invited her to come to his palace. She had never met Hussein, who always claimed to be too busy to meet ambassadors in recent years. At last she could meet him and try to find out what Hussein really wanted.

KUWAIT INVADED

During spring and summer 1990, Saddam Hussein increased his pressure on Kuwait. He demanded that Kuwait stop drilling near the disputed oil field at Rumaila. He reiterated his demands for a lease on the island that blocked his short shoreline on the gulf. As a result of his war with Iran, sunken ships blocked Iraq's port on the gulf, Umm Qasr, and he desperately needed new access to the sea to maintain and expand his country's oil exports.

The fact that Saudi Arabia and the United States had quietly supported his regime during the long war with Iran appeared to give Hussein a sense of assurance that those two countries would accept his aggressive pressures on Kuwait. And in 1989 and 1990, the Soviet Union was preoccupied with anticommunist upheavals, elections, and revolutions in its neighboring countries in eastern Europe. Throughout the world, observers believed that the fall of the Berlin Wall in November 1989 signaled the end of Soviet dominance in eastern Europe.

Several events during 1990 may have helped convince Hussein that he had nothing to fear from opposition from the United States. On February 15, 1990, Voice of America, the U.S. government-controlled radio program, included an editorial about the overthrow of dictators who used secret police and terror to maintain control. The focus of the editorial was the country of Romania, which had just thrown out its longtime Communist dictator, Nicolae Ceaușescu, in December 1989. In a passing reference, the Voice of America radio editorial stated that secret police "still operate in China, North Korea, Iran, Iraq, Syria, Cuba, and Albania."

Although the editorial did not have much to do with Iraq, an official in Hussein's Foreign Ministry angrily called in the U.S. ambassador to Iraq, April Glaspie. The Iraqi protested America's interference in Iraq's affairs. Glaspie reported the heated comments back to the U.S. State Department, which ordered her to apologize to the Iraqi government.

She returned to the Foreign Ministry in Baghdad to deliver her message. She later explained to the U.S. Congress precisely what she had said in her conferences with Iraqi leaders. "My government regrets that the wording of the editorial left it open to incorrect interpretation," she said. She went on to add, "President Bush wants good relations with Iraq, relations built on confidence." Ambassador Glaspie's comments were exactly in line with her instructions. Meanwhile, the U.S. State Department criticized the Voice of America and made sure that the State Department would clear all future editorials that even mentioned Iraq. Official U.S. policy in early 1990 remained tilted toward Iraq.

Hussein continued to believe that the United States would never act to oppose him, and, as far as official U.S. policy went, that appeared to be true. At a meeting of Arab states later in February 1990, Hussein pointed out to his Arab colleagues that the United States had pulled out of Lebanon after terrorists killed 241 U.S. Marines there on October 23, 1983. He argued that the U.S. troops could never have captured Panamanian dictator Manuel Noriega in early 1990 if the Panamanians had put up a stiffer resistance. In short, he claimed America was no longer a threat to Arabian control of Arabian lands or Arabian oil. The tiger had become a pussycat, he believed.

When Iraq threatened Kuwait over the oil revenue question at an OPEC meeting in July 1990, Hussein moved 30,000 troops within Iraq to the border with Kuwait to back up his threats with a show of force. Kuwait and the United Arab Emirates immediately agreed to limit their pumping of oil and promised not to cheat on the production quotas. They agreed to support a rise in the price of crude oil. It appeared that Hussein's military threat had worked. In late July, he sent another 70,000 troops to the border area.

Hussein called Ambassador Glaspie to meet with him on July 25, 1990. It was the first time the Iraqis had invited her to meet their president since she arrived in the country. Hussein accused the U.S. State Department and the Central Intelligence Agency of plotting against him. He reminded Ambassador Glaspie about the so-called Vietnam syndrome, under which the American public appeared to be reluctant to send troops overseas.

"Yours is a society," he said, "that cannot accept 10,000 dead in one battle."

She remained calm and did not take his remarks as threatening. She stuck with the policy line that was in her instructions, assuring Hus-

U.S., French, and Italian troops patrol Beirut, Lebanon, during an unsuccessful peacekeeping mission in 1982. Hussein believed that the U.S. pullout there showed that Americans would not continue a mission with too many deaths of U.S. troops. *(DOD Defense Information Center, March ARB, California)*

sein that President Bush sought a good relationship with Iraq. She also pointed out that the United States did not have any position on disputes between two Arab countries. She said that she hoped the disagreements with Kuwait could be resolved quickly. Hussein had her remarks tape-recorded and released them later, in a way that made it seem that she had said it was OK to attack Kuwait, much to the embarrassment of the U.S. government.

Later, a committee of the U.S. Congress asked Glaspie to explain the conversation. She claimed the tape had been edited. She said she had asked that the dispute with Kuwait be resolved *peacefully,* but she agreed that she had not warned Hussein that the United States would meet an attack on Kuwait with an armed response. She had no such instructions.

There were many warning signs. Iraqi troops began to mass on the Iraqi side of the border with Kuwait. Hussein made official and unofficial hostile comments about the United States. Hussein continued to demand more concessions from Kuwait. Despite all these developments,

President Bush and the U.S. State Department continued to maintain a calm response to events right up to the day of the Iraqi invasion, August 2, 1990.

A week after the discussion with Glaspie, Hussein ordered his troops into Kuwait. At first, President Bush and Secretary of State James Baker assumed that the invasion would move into a few border areas and perhaps seize the island in the gulf to give Iraq better access to the sea. But as the invasion rolled right into Kuwait City, they realized that they had miscalculated.

Suddenly it appeared that Saddam Hussein was attempting to swallow up Kuwait entirely, as German dictator Adolf Hitler had swallowed up Austria, Czechoslovakia, and other territories in Europe some 50 years before. In the 1930s, Britain and France had attempted to maintain peace by quietly accepting most of Hitler's bluster and his seizures of territory. The parallels struck George Bush. He was a veteran of World War II, and he later compared Hussein with Hitler several times. Bush, whose speaking style sometimes made him the butt of stand-up comics, soon referred to Saddam Hussein by mispronouncing his name. Instead of "Sah-Dom," as most newscasters pronounced it, Bush would call the Iraqi dictator "Sad-Damn."

Although Baker and Bush realized that they had miscalculated by appeasing Hussein as the British and French had done with Hitler, it was also true that Hussein had miscalculated. He believed that the United States and other countries would let him make his move into Kuwait without any military response. Although Western sources had no clear clues as to his ultimate goals, many analysts believed that Hussein intended to continue his advance into Saudi Arabia and perhaps to seize the lands of Bahrain and the United Arab Emirates. If the United States took no action, there would be little to stop him.

The Iraqi invasion of Kuwait itself took only one day to complete, although scattered resistance by some armed Kuwaitis continued for weeks. Kuwaiti civilians woke up on the morning of August 2, 1990, to find Iraqi troops occupying their capital city. Soon troops began stealing from individuals and shops and at the same time rounding up military-age Kuwaiti men and shipping them off to prison camps.

The Iraqis emptied Kuwaiti hospitals of their civilian patients to make room for wounded Iraqis, shot by scattered resistance troops. Again and again, Iraqi soldiers entered private homes, stole any food or money they could, and then methodically raped the women and girls

Downtown Kuwait City reflected the oil wealth of the country, resembling a modern and prosperous American or European community. Here the streets stood deserted after the Iraqi invasion. *(DOD Defense Information Center, March ARB, California)*

they found. The troops also sought out the homes of the ruling family and burned those homes to the ground. The brutality continued as the Iraq troops fanned out to control the country. Meanwhile, thousands of Kuwaiti civilians, those with cars or other transport, tried to flee from the country. Some made it, while others were stopped on the road and robbed of all their money and sometimes their cars. Teenage boys were taken from their families to be sent off to camps. In some cases, parents were forcibly taken from their cars to be shot, leaving small children and infants in the cars in the desert sun.

Although the Iraqis seized the local radio stations and newspapers, word of their atrocities soon leaked out. For a few days, telephone lines to nearby countries remained open, and Kuwaitis sent out faxed reports of what was going on. Then, the flood of refugees brought more stories of the horrors that had happened to their peaceable kingdom, gathered and reported by journalist Jean P. Sasson in a small book entitled *The Rape of Kuwait.*

Yehina Hamza, a Kuwaiti newspaperman, reported, "The newspaper staff was horrified to witness the Iraqis surround and kill more than 300 Kuwaiti soldiers at the Ministry of Defense. The Kuwaitis had surrendered. They were slaughtered." The Iraqis caught and tortured Nizar, a Kuwaiti resistance leader, trying to get him to reveal the names of others fighting against them. He pleaded ignorance, and after two days they released him, thinking he knew nothing of the resistance. Within weeks, he got word to the outside world: "We are a small country but we are willing to fight. Let us walk first into the battle, into Saddam's bullets. We will die. But someone will have to come behind to take the land . . . We accept death. Help us, please."

The invasion happened so rapidly and the small country was taken so suddenly that there was no opportunity for any foreign powers to come to the assistance of Kuwait, even if there had been any willingness to do so. The first reaction, however, was one of shock and disbelief. On the day of the invasion, President Bush was in Colorado, meeting with British prime minister Margaret Thatcher. Thatcher

Immediately after the Iraqi invasion of Kuwait on August 2, 1990, President Bush met with his National Security Advisors to review the situation. Shown here are William Webster, Robert Kimmitt, Secretary Cheney, Richard Darman, Chief of Staff Sununu, Attorney General Richard Thornburgh, Nicholas Brady, Vice President Quayle, Gen. Colin Powell, Secretary James Watkins, and President Bush. *(George Bush Presidential Library)*

REFUGEES FROM KUWAIT

When Iraq invaded Kuwait, refugees flooded out of Kuwait, including large numbers of guest workers from other countries, as well as Kuwaitis and the relatively small number of European and Americans working there. At the start of the war there were at least 2 million foreign workers in the country. An estimated 700,000 guest workers fled to Jordan to be evacuated home. India and Pakistan flew most of their workers home. Of the 700,000 to 800,000 Kuwaiti citizens, about half fled the country, traveling overland to Jordan or Saudi Arabia.

Iraqi troops stopped those who drove in their own cars across Iraq to the Iraqi-Jordanian border. Along the way, some were accosted and shot, while others had their vehicles stolen. At the border, in a line of more than 1,000 cars, the Iraqi soldiers moved from car to car, stealing possessions.

For many Kuwaitis and guest workers, Jordan was only a temporary stop where they arranged flights either home or to a country of refuge. But for those who could not afford an air ticket or for whom no relief agency provided transport, the destination was one of 17 Jordanian refugee camps. After the first month of the invasion of Kuwait by Iraq, more than 100,000 refugees remained in the camps.

Many Kuwaiti citizens flew to Egypt, where there was already a wealthy Kuwaiti colony and where some owned homes or had relatives. The Kuwaiti embassy in Egypt became a clearinghouse for information about Kuwaiti refugees. Some who escaped with no money and no funds in Egypt, as well as children separated from their parents, lived on the embassy grounds. There, many of the refugees recounted for social workers, medical personnel, and journalists the horrors and atrocities they had faced before leaving Kuwait.

said she would stand by the United States in stopping Hussein. While Thatcher and Bush discussed the situation, King Fahd of Saudi Arabia called President Bush on the phone.

Fahd was stunned. Only a few days before, Hussein had assured Fahd that he would not move against Kuwait. Fahd wondered if the United States would send troops to protect Saudi Arabia. He asked whether the troops would go home as soon as the threat of an invasion of Saudi Arabia was eliminated. He also asked whether the United States would step up its sale of advanced weapons to Saudi Arabia.

George Bush said he agreed to all three propositions, and Fahd said he would need to consider the situation.

By the second day, August 3, 1990, Iraqi troops were already within five miles of Kuwait's border with Saudi Arabia. The situation was desperate. The Saudis had only 65,000 troops, while Hussein reportedly had an army of 1 million, with about 100,000 moving through Kuwait directly toward the Saudi border. President Bush and his advisers recognized that stopping Hussein was more than a military question. Even if enough U.S. troops could be flown to Saudi Arabia within a few days to slow the Iraqi advance and prevent Hussein from seizing northern oil fields, that solution would not work for many political reasons.

At the end of the war, some Kuwaiti prisoners held in Iraq were repatriated by air. *(Defense Imagery)*

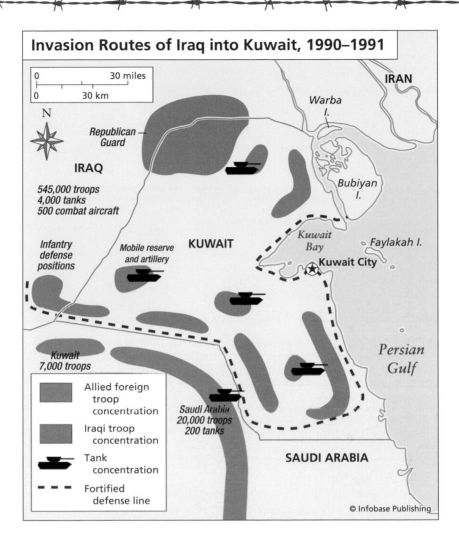

Invasion Routes of Iraq into Kuwait, 1990–1991

0   30 miles

0   30 km

N

Republican Guard

IRAN

Warba I.

IRAQ

545,000 troops
4,000 tanks
500 combat aircraft

Bubiyan I.

Infantry defense positions

Mobile reserve and artillery

KUWAIT

Kuwait Bay

Faylakah I.

Kuwait City

Kuwait
7,000 troops

Persian Gulf

Allied foreign troop concentration

Iraqi troop concentration

Tank concentration

Fortified defense line

Saudi Arabia
20,000 troops
200 tanks

SAUDI ARABIA

© Infobase Publishing

If only the United States, or the United States and Britain together, came to the aid of Saudi Arabia, such an action could unite Arabs on Hussein's side. Many Arabs saw the United States as the friend of Israel, providing one reason for suspicion of U.S. goals. Furthermore, if the conflict looked like one only between Europeans and Arabs, or only between Christians and Muslims, the bond of Arab brotherhood would come into play. It would seem as if the Europeans wanted to prevent Arab control of Arab land and Arab oil. The region's people remembered the long heritage of British control in the region as well as the tradition of U.S. support for Israel, and they understood the deep differences between the strict moral code of Islam and the cultural

On November 1, 1988, U.S. Secretary of Defense Frank C. Carlucci *(center)* transferred the command of the U.S. Central Command from General George B. Crist, USMC (left), to Gen. Norman Schwarzkopf. *(Defense Imagery)*

freedoms of the United States and Britain. However, if a broader base of support could be built, including Arabs and perhaps even the Soviet Union and its former satellites, then there was a chance that Hussein could be stopped.

In November 1988 General Schwarzkopf had taken command of the U.S. Central Command (CENTCOM), the Defense Department's designation for U.S. forces to be deployed to the region that included Saudi Arabia and the Persian Gulf. Months before the Iraqi invasion Schwarzkopf had worked up a plan to increase forces in CENTCOM and had developed, as an exercise, the requirements for a 150,000-troop deployment. At CENTCOM headquarters in Tampa, Florida, he had just conducted exercises with his officers over the plan, code-named "Internal Look." The plan envisioned an unnamed dictator attempting to seize the oil resources of the Persian Gulf. The plan was ready to go, but to use that plan without full Arab support would never work.

Within a week, Schwarzkopf had his orders: Go to Saudi Arabia, begin the buildup, and stop Hussein if he invaded. Operation Desert Shield was under way by August 9, 1990.

OPERATION
DESERT SHIELD

A Line in the Sand

The mission faced by General Schwarzkopf evolved over time. At first he had to quickly put enough forces in place to discourage the Iraqis from attempting to cross from conquered Kuwait into Saudi Arabia. Schwarzkopf had two plans available to show to President Bush and his advisers. One plan showed the troops needed to defend Saudi Arabia, and the second plan showed the forces needed to liberate Kuwait. The second plan would have to wait.

In the first months, through August and September 1990, those close to President Bush realized that if the Iraqis threw their forces in the region into an assault, the Americans and Saudis would have to fight a rearguard action. Some even compared the defenders' role to that of the South Korean and American troops who fell back in the first months of the Korean War to the Pusan perimeter and then held that area until further reinforcements could arrive. For a defense to prevent such a situation, a huge force would be needed.

Although the Saudi government had lots of advanced equipment, including new fighter aircraft and radar-surveillance and reconnaissance aircraft, it had only 65,000 troops, no match for the Iraqi forces. Schwarzkopf's first defensive plan called for two divisions of U.S. soldiers, a combat brigade, 500 aircraft, and naval support including several aircraft carriers. Altogether, he envisioned at least 150,000 American troops, just for a defense of Saudi Arabia.

The U.S. Defense Department issued the first orders for deployment on August 6. Several long-range B-52 bomber aircraft were shuttled to the American base on the island of Diego Garcia in the Indian

Gen. Colin Powell, chairman of the Joint Chiefs of Staff, greets crew members aboard the battleship USS *Wisconsin* while visiting the ship during Operation Desert Shield. On his right is Vice Adm. Michael P. Kalleres. *(Defense Imagery)*

Ocean, and two squadrons of F-15 fighters were deployed to the gulf to be based in Saudi Arabia.

Building the force was a matter of logistics, troop movement, establishing quarters, and bringing up weapons. The job was made difficult by conditions in Saudi Arabia. In August, the daytime temperature rose to 130°F. Equipment had to be redesigned. Even the boots worn by GIs were unsuitable—they had vents to allow water to drain out, and in Saudi Arabia those holes allowed sand to creep in. The brown-and-green woodland camouflage uniforms appropriate for Europe had to be exchanged for a tan, yellow, and brown desert camouflage suited for the desert. Airstrips and storage areas had to be constructed, and hundreds of thousands of tons of equipment and supplies had to be assembled.

Schwarzkopf, who had lived overseas for a few years as a child, including a stay in Tehran, Iran, knew it was important that U.S. troops respect local culture. Military chaplains cooperated, avoiding public services and presenting themselves as counselors rather than as priests, ministers, and rabbis. Troops avoided alcohol and female entertainment. When an officer complained that the troops' constitutional rights were being violated, Schwarzkopf pointed out that the U.S. Constitution did not apply to Arabia and that as guests of the country, his forces had to obey local law.

The logistics were difficult, but in some ways the diplomatic side was even more difficult. Without support from Arab states, putting thousands of U.S. troops into Saudi Arabia would backfire, winning support for Hussein from Arabs everywhere. Hussein would be able to claim that Americans had invaded Saudi Arabia. Popular movements in Egypt, the Persian Gulf states, and elsewhere would threaten to overthrow established governments, swinging them suddenly into support for Iraq.

President Bush worked for diplomatic support on several fronts. One was through his personal contacts with world leaders, contacts that he had carefully built up over his years as vice president under Ronald Reagan (1981–89) and in his first year as president. Calmly, Bush went on an August "vacation" to Kennebunkport, Maine, and while there placed more than 60 phone calls to world leaders.

LOGISTICS
Why the Long Wait?

One of the reasons that Operation Desert Shield lasted from August 1990 to mid-January 1991 was simply that it took a long time to mount the invasion. Although the time allowed an opportunity for diplomacy and for congressional consideration, it was necessary to get sufficient supplies on the ground before taking action against Iraq. In military terminology, the science of supplying equipment, food, weapons, ammunition, vehicles, and temporary shelter is called "logistics." General Schwarzkopf entrusted much of the logistics of supplying material for more than 560,000 U.S. troops to Maj. Gen. William (Gus) Pagonis, who was a master at the game.

As Schwarzkopf remembered, Pagonis pulled it all together from scratch, including post offices and field clinics. He provided phone booths for soldiers to call home. He set up recreational facilities and hamburger stands. He scrounged from the Saudi government tents that were available for the annual pilgrimage of the faithful to Mecca. The result was that American troops were about as comfortable as any soldiers could be during a war.

Meanwhile, he worked through formal channels. On the day of the Iraqi invasion, the U.S. ambassador to the United Nations, Thomas Pickering, led an effort to pass a Security Council resolution condemning the invasion and calling for an Iraqi withdrawal. Secretary of State James Baker was in Mongolia, and he flew home by way of Moscow, where he obtained a promise that the Soviets would assist in an embargo of Iraq, although it could not directly support a military action. In addition, Soviet foreign minister Eduard Shevardnadze pledged not to supply the Iraqis with weapons or with spare parts for equipment. Baker and Shevardnadze issued a joint statement condemning Hussein's invasion and asking other countries to join in an embargo of Iraq.

On August 6, the UN Security Council passed a stronger resolution than their first, asking member nations to support an embargo against Iraq. Even before the UN embargo, U.S. ships blockaded Iraqi oil tankers that came through the Persian Gulf. But a United Nations resolution condemning the Iraqi invasion and support for an embargo from the Soviet Union and the United Nations were not enough. To build up Middle Eastern and Arab support, Bush began with Turkey and Egypt.

President George H. W. Bush being formally received by King Fahd on his arrival in Jeddah, Saudi Arabia, on November 21, 1990. Bush was there to express the full commitment of the United States to the territory of Saudi Arabia as well as Kuwait. (*George Bush Presidential Library*)

Secretary Baker flew to Turkey to provide assurances to that government. Turkey depended on Iraq for about half of its oil supply, and a major part of its revenue came from a pipeline that crossed Turkey from Iraq. In any embargo of Iraq, Turkey could lose billions of dollars a year. The emir of Kuwait promised financial aid to Turkey. Baker told Turkish president Turgut Osal that member nations of the North Atlantic Treaty Organization (NATO), including the United States, Canada, and their western European allies, as well as Turkey, would come to his aid if Iraq took military action against the Turks. President Osal agreed to enforce the embargo and to allow the United States to base more aircraft at Incirlik, a bomber base in Turkey. Help from Turkey was essential, because Iraq would then be forced to tie down troops at its border with Turkey.

Other Middle Eastern countries also feared both political and economic disaster if they came to the aid of Kuwait. President Bush worked directly with the president of Egypt, Hosni Mubarak. As part of an earlier peace treaty between Israel and Egypt, the United States provided more than $2 billion a year to the Egyptian government in military and economic aid. However, Egypt faced a special economic problem. An estimated 1 million Egyptians worked in Iraq and about 300,000 worked in Kuwait.

If Egypt went to war against Iraq, those Egyptians would be at risk. At the least, the money they earned in wages and sent home would be cut off. Bush told Mubarak that he would ask the U.S. Congress to cancel an outstanding debt of more than $6 billion that Egypt owed to America. The Egyptians agreed to help. They would send 5,000 soldiers, they would allow the United States to fly through Egyptian airspace, and they would allow warships destined for the Persian Gulf to go through the Egyptian-controlled Suez Canal. In addition, Mubarak agreed to help round up further Arab support.

Syria was another difficult partner. The United States had long suspected that Syria supported international terrorists. Syria had fought several wars against Israel and supported anti-Israeli forces in Lebanon. Israel occupied the Golan Heights, a border zone inside Syria, and Israel and Syria had not made formal peace with each other. On the other hand, Syria and Iraq had a long-standing enmity, and Syria had supported Iran during the 1980s Iran-Iraq war. To encourage support, several of the wealthy Persian Gulf states pledged to provide foreign aid to Syria, estimated in the range of $2 billion to $3 billion. Syria agreed to supply troops for the effort against Iraq and to join in the embargo against Iraq. Syria's support was vital, as Syria and Iraq shared more than 400 miles of border.

The coalition-building among Arabs was under way. The smaller states of the Persian Gulf—Qatar, Bahrain, the United Arab Emirates, and Oman—felt more directly threatened by the Iraqi invasion and pledged both military and financial support. The United States politely rejected offers of assistance from Israel, as few Arab leaders would have been able to explain to their people why they fought alongside Israel against a brother Arab state.

Although Japan was dependent on the region for oil, and in fact more dependent than any other major industrial nation, its constitution prohibited the use of its military forces for any role except self-defense. Consequently, Japan limited its participation in the Coalition to monetary support. South Korea, long dependent on U.S. troop presence to deter an invasion from North Korea, and also dependent on Middle Eastern oil, agreed to financial support.

Eventually, 34 nations pledged some form of military support and another 14 provided financial or other aid. For the United States, France, Britain, Saudi Arabia, Syria, and Egypt, military participation meant putting troops on the ground. Britain, France, Saudi Arabia, and the United States supplied aircraft and pilots. Other countries sent specialized military units, naval ships to assist in the blockade, or military medical teams. In the case of about five or six of the Coalition partners, their participation was so slight they were not always included in lists of member states.

Holding the Coalition together was not simple. The longer the Coalition based itself on strictly defensive lines, the more impatient member states became. On the other hand, if President Bush hinted too strongly that he intended to change the mission from defense to liberation, some members of the Coalition might drop out.

As U.S. forces increased in Saudi Arabia, the Iraqis increased the numbers of their own forces in Kuwait and near the Saudi border. By the end of October, the United States had 210,000 troops in the region, backing up the 65,000 Saudis. In addition, other Coalition members began to send units. However, the Iraqi forces had increased from about 100,000 to more than 400,000 in Kuwait in the same period. Even a believable defense by the Coalition would have to be far larger.

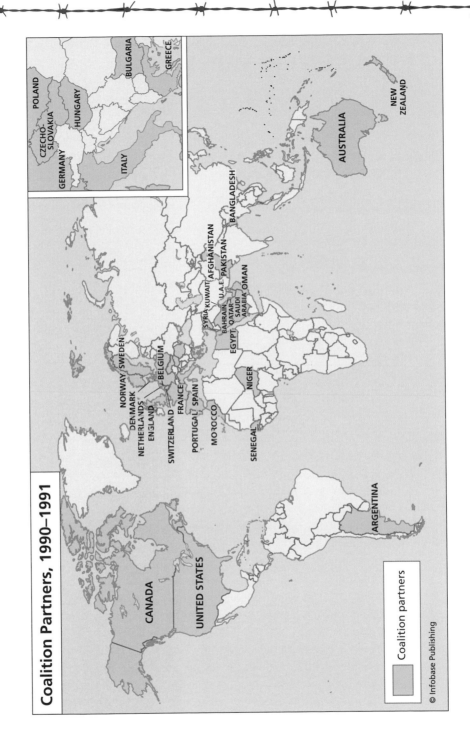

Coalition Partners, 1990–1991

BULGARIA
GREECE
POLAND
CZECHO-
SLOVAKIA
HUNGARY
GERMANY
ITALY

NEW
ZEALAND
AUSTRALIA

BANGLADESH
AFGHANISTAN
SYRIA KUWAIT PAKISTAN
U.A.E.
BAHRAIN OMAN
QATAR SAUDI
EGYPT ARABIA
NIGER

NORWAY SWEDEN
DENMARK BELGIUM
NETHERLANDS
ENGLAND
SWITZERLAND FRANCE
PORTUGAL SPAIN
MOROCCO
SENEGAL

CANADA

UNITED STATES

ARGENTINA

Coalition partners

© Infobase Publishing

THE COALITION PARTNERS

To enforce the United Nations Resolution 678, many nations formed a coalition to evict Iraq from Kuwait. The Arab nations of Kuwait, Egypt, Saudi Arabia, Morocco, Bahrain, Oman, Syria, and Qatar participated in the Coalition. Some of the countries that had once been satellite nations of the Soviet Union during the cold war also joined the Coalition. Thirty-four countries provided military help. They all served under the centralized command of Gen. Norman Schwarzkopf and Gen. Khalid Sultan of Saudi Arabia.

The full list of the 34 countries providing military units was as follows:

Afghanistan	France	Pakistan
(rebels)	Germany	Poland
Argentina	Greece	Portugal
Australia	Hungary	Qatar
Bahrain	Italy	Saudi Arabia
Bangladesh	Kuwait	Senegal
Belgium	Morocco	Spain
Britain	Netherlands	Sweden
Canada	New Zealand	Syria
Czech Republic	Niger	United Arab
Denmark	Norway	Emirates
Egypt	Oman	United States

Although Turkey did not send troops, the presence of Turkish troops near that country's border with Iraq helped divert Iraqi forces. Some of the countries supplied only token forces or small units that had special duties such as mine clearing or dealing with poison gas. But a number made major contributions. The United States, France, Britain, and Saudi Arabia all provided aircraft and pilots. Egypt sent a mechanized division and an armored division. In addition, another 18 nations gave economic, humanitarian, or other forms of assistance.

When Schwarzkopf's command set up transport, it included caravans of trucks from many nations, including some from Poland, Germany, and the Czech Republic, often with drivers from Bangladesh or Pakistan. The Coalition drew personnel from every continent except Antarctica.

In late October, Gen. Colin Powell visited Schwarzkopf to discuss the problem. Schwarzkopf told Powell that an offensive plan would require at least 400,000 American troops. If the president approved, and if troops could continue to arrive at the predicted rate, Schwarzkopf explained, sufficient forces would be in place by mid-January 1991 to shift from defense to offense. Bush gave the go-ahead for the continued buildup.

But to make the shift from defense to offense, Bush had several tough diplomatic hurdles ahead. First, he had to secure the agreement of the Coalition partners, some of whom had entered only on the grounds of defending Saudi Arabia. Second, he would need a strengthened endorsement from the United Nations, some kind of justification under international law for waging war, not simply positioning defensive forces. Third, and perhaps most difficult, he would need some form of support in the U.S. Congress.

Bush and his advisers carefully timed all of these moves. During November, the United States would hold the rotating chairmanship of the UN Security Council. Although the United States had only one

U.S. Marines "hurry up and wait" to board naval ships for transport to Saudi Arabia during Desert Shield. *(DOD Defense Information Center, March ARB, California)*

vote in that group, the chair could steer discussion. On November 6, the United States would hold congressional elections. Rather than throw the issue of switching from defense to offense into the political arena, Bush decided to hold off his actions until mid- or late November. Meantime, he intentionally gave mixed messages in his public statements.

Some of Bush's political critics took his dual messages as a sign of his often confusing style of speaking rather than any intentional pattern. He claimed that he wanted to give sanctions time to work, but then said that the "sand is running through the glass" for Hussein. When he announced the troop buildup, he claimed it was to give more force to the pressure on Hussein, not to prepare for invasion. Then Bush hinted that the troops would provide an offensive capacity, if required. The lack of clarity was at least partly intentional, keeping Hussein unsure and at the same time not scaring away Coalition supporters who feared that a switch in strategy would result in a tragic defeat.

As Bush began to hint at a possible offensive war, antiwar demonstrations and political opposition began to build in the United States. Senator Sam Nunn, chair of the Armed Services Committee, ordered hearings into U.S. policy in the Persian Gulf. Nunn called a series of former cabinet officers and chairs of the Joint Chiefs of Staff, asking their opinions. Almost all of them agreed that the United States should continue to back the defensive strategy. They argued for patience and time enough to make the embargo work.

Bush and Secretary Baker then began lining up support for a new UN resolution. The United Nations had already issued 11 resolutions against Iraq, but a stronger 12th resolution could authorize the use of force. At a meeting in November in Paris, Bush worked with leaders from European countries to ask for support at the United Nations for such a resolution, getting agreement from Britain but reluctance from France and Russia.

Baker and Bush continued to make contacts. Bush visited U.S. troops in Saudi Arabia on Thanksgiving, and then he went on to Syria. Baker visited other countries that held temporary seats on the UN Security Council. On November 29, toward the end of the U.S. chairmanship of the council, the United States secured passage of UN Resolution 678. The resolution authorized the use of force if the Iraqis did not withdraw from Kuwait by January 15, 1991. The resolution passed with no negative votes and only Cuba and Yemen abstaining.

On November 22, 1990, during the Thanksgiving weekend, President and Mrs. Bush, here walking in the desert of Saudi Arabia with Gen. Schwarzkopf and an entourage, visited the U.S. troops. *(George Bush Presidential Library)*

Between the first of December 1990 and the middle of January 1991 Arab and European diplomats launched various peace initiatives to try to work out some sort of compromise. To stop the various efforts, Bush sent Baker to meet with Iraqi foreign minister Tariq Aziz in Geneva, Switzerland, on January 9 to deliver an ultimatum. Aziz refused to deliver a letter from Bush to Hussein. The Iraqis did not believe the United States and the Coalition would attack. Baker reported that no progress had been made. The deadline neared.

Baker flew from Geneva to Saudi Arabia to inform King Fahd, who gave him approval to begin an air war launched from Saudi airfields following the January 15 deadline. Then, on January 12, Bush asked Congress for a resolution to support the use of force. In voting watched by millions of Americans on television, the House of Representatives approved by a vote of 250 to 183, the Senate approved by a closer 52 to 47. On the whole, most Republicans supported the resolution, and the Democrats split, with 10 out of 55 Democratic senators and 86 out of 265 Democratic representatives joining Republican colleagues to vote

On January 15, 1991, on the eve of commencing Operation Desert Storm, George Bush met with his top advisers: (from left to right) Robert Gates, John Sununu, Richard Cheney, Dan Quayle, President Bush, James Baker, Brent Scowcroft, and Colin Powell. *(Defense Imagery)*

for military action. The close Senate vote, Bush thought, was the most tension-filled moment of the crisis.

President Bush had aligned the forces, military, diplomatic, and political. The deadline of January 15 came and went.

Then on January 16, the air war began. Americans watched their television screens as cameras in Baghdad caught the detonations of cruise missiles and bombs and the spectacular lines of antiaircraft fire from the ground.

Operation Desert Shield had become Operation Desert Storm.

THE AIR WAR AND PRELIMINARY GROUND ACTIVITIES

Operation Desert Storm began on the night of January 16/17, 1991. It was 6:35 P.M. in the evening of January 16 on the East Coast of the United States. It was 2:35 A.M. in the morning of January 17 in Baghdad when F-117 Stealth bombers aimed precise laser-guided bombs at key targets in that city. Coordinated air strikes and Tomahawk cruise missiles launched from the USS *Wisconsin* and USS *Missouri* in the Persian Gulf sought out targets such as communication centers, airports, missile launching sites, and oil refineries. It was the first time that the Tomahawks had ever been used in warfare.

The instantaneous medium of television allowed viewers to watch the first minutes of the battle broadcast live from Baghdad. Although other reporters and television crews were hustled from their hotel rooms and prevented from broadcasting, Cable News Network (CNN) reporters Peter Arnett and Bernard Shaw managed to stay on, remaining in their room. The television network started by Atlanta businessman Ted Turner in 1980 had taken on the traditional networks, presenting 24-hour news broadcasts with both world coverage and world audiences. CNN had about 100 staff members in the Persian Gulf region when the war started. Audiences in some 105 countries around the world viewed the CNN reports. Arnett and Shaw described the first battles simply by phoning in their reports, standing by their hotel windows and then holding the phones out to catch the noise of detonations. Their camera operator escaped detention by claiming a heart condition; he then ran up many flights of stairs to join his colleagues in their room. The CNN crew kept broadcasting for 16 hours, before Iraqi authorities finally stopped them. Later, the Iraqis allowed Arnett and a few other newspeople to view damage and to interview casualties, but they maintained tight control over the news crews.

One of the first goals of the air strikes was to make sure the Iraqis turned on their radar defense system, so that special missiles launched from British and American aircraft could lock on and destroy the radar installations. Another early goal was to track down and destroy the ground-to-ground missiles known as Scuds that the Iraqis had acquired. With the radar incapacitated within two hours, Iraqi antiaircraft fire and surface-to-air missiles streaked skyward in uncoordinated bursts. Even so, the United States lost a total of 27 aircraft in the war and could say with certainty that 11 losses had been due to antiaircraft fire and one to a surface-to-air missile. Tracking the Scuds, many of which were mounted on mobile truck launchers, was far more difficult.

In the first air raids, American, British, French, Saudi, and Kuwaiti pilots flew from bases in Saudi Arabia, Turkey, and the Gulf States (Qatar, Bahrain, and the United Arab Emirates) as well as from aircraft carriers in the Persian Gulf. British aircraft targeted airfields with special concrete-busting bombs, while the French struck an Iraqi military airfield near Kuwait City. With the outbreak of the attack, however, various Coalition nations put limits on their participation. Italian warships would only attack targets inside Kuwait. The Netherlands limited its participation to two frigates and no ground troops. Portugal and Spain limited their ships to blockade duty. Spain, despite powerful antiwar sentiments in its population, continued to allow U.S. B-52s to use the air base at Moron, Spain, for bombing raids over Iraq. Other U.S. air bases in Spain played an important part in transporting supplies and U.S. troops to Iraq.

Measured by sorties (a sortie being a single flight by one aircraft), on the first day the U.S.-led forces made massive strikes from 2,000 sorties and hits by more than 100 Tomahawk missiles. In the first 14 hours, only three U.S. aircraft were lost, all to ground fire. In fact, during the total air war and later ground campaign, the Coalition lost only 46 aircraft, none to enemy aircraft attacks. U.S. forces flew more than 75,000 sorties, two-thirds by the U.S. Air Force, and the rest by the U.S. Navy and U.S. Marines. The total sorties do not include helicopter missions.

On the second night of fighting, the Iraqis fired their first Scud missiles toward Israel, with six hitting in the city of Tel Aviv and at

Military personnel are examining the tail section of an Iraqi Scud missile shot down in the desert by a Patriot tactical air defense missile during Operation Desert Storm. *(Defense Imagery)*

least one in Haifa. Fearing a poison gas attack, many Israelis put on gas masks and taped up windows and doors to block out the poison. However, all the Scuds carried conventional high explosive. U.S. officials negotiated to keep the Israelis from retaliating on the Scud sites in western Iraq.

According to the *New York Times,* an American senior official called Israel. "We are going after western Iraq full bore," the American said. "There is nothing that your air force can do that we are not already doing. If there is, tell us and we will do it. . . . Please don't play into Saddam's hands." The Israelis reportedly called back aircraft they had scrambled (put into action). The United States intensified "Scud-hunting" and at the same time made plans to ship two Patriot antimissile batteries to Israel. Meanwhile, Islamic religious leaders and newspapers in Saudi Arabia carefully downplayed any news of the Scud attacks on Israel and the U.S. response of sending Patriot missiles there.

As the bombing and missile attacks continued, it soon became clear that the Coalition military forces had a larger goal than simply driving the Iraqis from Kuwait. Targets included Iraqi nuclear research facilities, defense plants, chemical weapons factories, and military targets. Furthermore, Coalition air strikes were aimed at eliminating the Iraqi

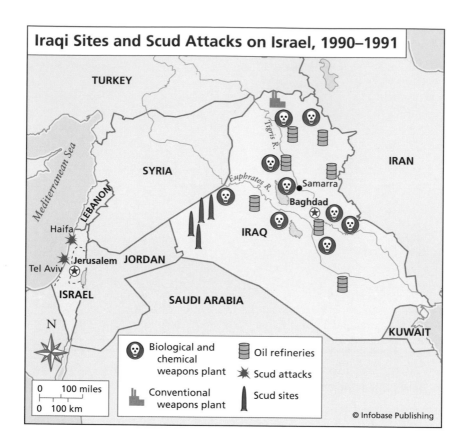

Iraqi Sites and Scud Attacks on Israel, 1990–1991

ability to communicate from headquarters to the field, by destroying power stations, radio and telephone facilities, and whole floors of important government buildings in downtown Baghdad. Airdrops also concentrated on Baathist Party headquarters and Hussein's hometown of Tikrit.

During the first two weeks of the air campaign, the United States and its allies dropped more explosives on Iraq and Kuwait than the Allies had used in six years of World War II. In fact, the total tonnage of explosives in the first night's attack (18,000 tons, or 18 kilotons), when combined, nearly equaled the explosive force of the atomic bomb dropped over Hiroshima, Japan, on August 6, 1945, estimated at 20 kilotons.

The air strikes not only weakened the command and control system that allowed Hussein to keep in touch with his officers in the field but they struck at the country's infrastructure as well. Raids knocked out bridges over the Tigris and Euphrates Rivers. Bombs repeatedly hit highways, pipelines, power lines, and Iraq's already-crippled seaport on the gulf.

Sometimes pilots returned to attack buildings that they had already turned into rubble, making larger rocks into smaller rocks, as the pilots said. The burning Dohra refinery on the edge of Baghdad sent up clouds of smoke visible from 60 miles away. In Iraq's second-largest town, Basra, the water supply was completely cut off. Even gasoline, in a country that had held about 10 percent of the world's petroleum reserves, had to be rationed. Authorities allowed each car about eight

A Tomahawk Land-Attack Missile is here being launched toward a target in Iraq from the guided missile cruiser USS *Mississippi*. Operation Desert Storm was the first time such a weapon was used in combat. *(Defense Imagery)*

gallons every 15 days. About 1 million Baghdad residents left the city, returning to villages or quietly leaving the country by way of Jordan.

The attacks on Baghdad and on other Iraqi targets continued. The incoming cruise missiles were an eerie sight. CNN correspondent Arnett saw one fly past his hotel room window, silently zeroing in on the Defense Ministry in Baghdad. American and British television began to show videotapes of some of the missile attacks from the point of view of the weapon itself. First, the tape showed how a laser beam marked a target, with crosshairs centering on a pinpoint of light. Then, the camera in the missile would take over, as the missile recorded its own approach to the target. In one strike, the top floors of an air-force building simply blew off after a missile hit. In other shots, a missile flew into an airshaft or into a specific window in a building.

SCUDS AND PATRIOTS

The Soviet SS-1 missile (surface-to-surface type 1) had a range of about 190 miles. The Iraqis made Scuds by welding two SS-1s together, increasing the range to more than 300 miles but decreasing the weapon's accuracy. The Iraqis could drive a truck-mounted Scud to a spot in the desert, set up, aim, and fire the missile in a short period.

On January 18, Iraq launched eight Scuds toward Israel. Six detonated in Tel Aviv and one, possibly two, in the town of Haifa. If the Israelis retaliated, the Arab members of the Coalition might withdraw, thereby breaking up the anti-Iraq front and weakening, even destroying, its international political base.

Although Israel had a plan to locate and destroy the Scud sites, U.S. officials pressured Israel to hold back. The United States promised to search out the Scuds and to provide new military aid to Israel. Waves of fighter-bombers fanned out over western Iraq, destroying Scud sites. Iraq sent more Scuds toward U.S. and Arab facilities in Riyadh and Dhahran in Saudi Arabia.

Americans based in Saudi Arabia fired Patriot antiaircraft missiles that intercepted and destroyed some of the Scuds. The United States also sent two groups of Patriot missiles with crews to Israel. Even so, one Scud later landed in Tel Aviv, injuring 90 people. Altogether an estimated 40 Scuds were aimed at Israel, 48 at Saudi Arabia, Qatar, and Bahrain. As the war neared its end, on February 25, a Scud traveled some 200 miles into Arabia, broke apart in flight, and hit a U.S.

Part of the reason for showing the highly accurate targeting was to decrease concerns about collateral damage, as damage to or injury or death of nonmilitary targets was known. Yet the Iraqi civilian casualties continued to mount. In one claim, Radio Baghdad announced that bombing raids on the town of Nasiriyah had killed 150 civilians, including 35 children. Independent sources could not verify the attack.

In the worst such incident of the war, on February 13, two U.S. F-117A fighterbombers attacked a reinforced bunkerlike structure in the Baghdad neighborhood of Amiriya. Photographs had shown that military vehicles and soldiers guarded the building. Furthermore, radio signals had indicated it was some sort of military facility. However, local civilians had been using the structure as a shelter. More than 400 civilians, including women and children, died in the

barracks near Dhahran. The missile killed 28 U.S. troops and injured about another 90.

After the war, analysts debated the Patriot's success against Scuds. Because the Scud was inaccurate in any case, large debris from the Patriot and Scud explosion could be as frightening and damaging as the original Scud.

A Patriot missile is fired from its mobile launcher. Although the Patriot had only mixed success against the Scud, it was the best antimissile missile that the United States could deploy at the time. (*Defense Imagery*)

wreckage. Signs in both Arabic and English posted on the building had designated it as an air-raid shelter. While the Iraqis claimed the attack as a planned atrocity, Coalition forces claimed that the Iraqis had intentionally placed a civilian shelter in a military facility. The Iraqis flooded the lower levels so that visiting newsmen had no way of verifying if a military command post was below the shelter. The tragedy weakened popular and governmental support for the air raids, even among European allies. Spain asked for an international investigation and a halt to attacks on targets in Baghdad. Many Americans were deeply shocked at the carnage.

Although the Tomahawk seemed like one of the high-tech weapons of the new type of war, and it had never been tried in warfare before, it had been in the U.S. arsenal for years. Even some of the Tomahawk missiles hit unintended targets. On February 1, five Tomahawks struck Baghdad. One landed in the residential neighborhood of Karada, among houses and shops. Another put a deep crater next to an outdoor swimming pool in the Masbah district. Neither site had military facilities nearby. More controversial was a hit at a factory at Abu Ghreib on the outskirts of Baghdad. The Iraqis claimed the factory produced infant formula. Western journalists toured the site and observed milk powder and containers and a pasteurizing line. The U.S. Defense Department claimed the factory had been disguised and that it really produced biological weapons.

In some cases, the Iraqis rigged evidence, once demolishing a mosque and claiming that an American bomb did the damage. In another case, a British television reporter found that some civilian casualties in a hospital were Iraqi soldiers, concealing parts of their uniforms under the bedclothes. Combined with genuine bombing mistakes, Iraqi propaganda began to have an effect not only in Spain and in Arab countries but in Britain and the United States as well.

The Coalition targeted military objectives, no matter how well hidden. By mid-February, less than a month after the raids began, the Coalition reported that its bombs and missiles had destroyed 1,300 of the Iraqi 4,280 tanks, 1,100 of 3,100 artillery pieces, and 850 of the 2,870 armored personnel carriers. Coalition forces destroyed 56 aircraft on the ground and 42 in air-to-air combat. Iraq ferried at least 140 aircraft to Iran, where they remained safe from attack for the duration of the war. By the end of the bombing campaign, Coalition air strikes began to number about 3,000 a day.

COLLATERAL DAMAGE

The American public became familiar with some military jargon and terminology during the Persian Gulf War. Often the terms seemed intended to conceal the ugliness of war behind polite phrases. Some of these have been in use for a long time. The chaotic confusion of the battlefield has been known as *the fog of war*. The accidental killing or injury of one's own or allied troops is referred to as *friendly fire*.

The phrase that most shocked the American public was *collateral damage*. The Defense Department used this expression to describe the unintended effect of a weapon strike against an intended target that had military or strategic significance. Thus, if a missile or bomb missed an important power station or bridge and fell on civilians, including schoolchildren or innocent shoppers in a market, their deaths would be called "collateral damage." Although pilots sought to avoid such tragedies, collateral damage in Iraq claimed thousands of lives.

U.S. and Saudi troops inspect the damage to an elementary school in Saudi Arabia hit by an Iraqi Scud missile, February 24, 1991. *(DOD Defense Information Center March ARB, California)*

Although successful in a military sense, the bombing raids stirred sympathy in other countries, not only for Iraqi civilians accidentally killed or injured, but also for the regime of Saddam Hussein itself. Morocco, a member of the Coalition, allowed an antiwar demonstration on February 3 that drew some 500,000 people. In Tunisia and Algeria, pro-Iraqi demonstrations showed public opinion decidedly in favor of the Iraqis. Even Syria, with its long history of enmity to Iraq, saw claims by Islamic groups that America was the invader. Egypt and Saudi Arabia reiterated that their forces would fight to liberate Kuwait but would not engage in warfare inside Iraq itself. Reports filtered out that in Saudi Arabia much of the population showed a grudging respect for Saddam Hussein and the Iraqi people as they stood up under the bombing raids.

Jordan remained officially neutral but continued its overland oil trade from Iraq by truck. When Coalition aircraft destroyed several tank trucks on February 4, the pilots claimed it was because the trucks seemed very similar to the mobile Scud-transport vehicles. Nevertheless, UN Secretary-General Pérez de Cuéllar took the opportunity to come to Jordan's defense, reported in the London *Independent* the next day. "Jordan is an innocent victim of what is happening," he said. "This is something inadmissible. . . . I do deplore these acts."

King Hussein of Jordan joined others in the Arab world in speaking out against the Coalition, claiming it resembled the agreements by which England and France had divided up the Ottoman Empire after World War I. The U.S. response to complaints about Jordanian truck and truck-driver losses was to declare the highway from Baghdad to Jordan's capital Amman a military target. In effect, the United States warned that peaceful traffic would travel at its own risk.

As the bombing raids wore on, Bush and the other Coalition leaders recognized that world opinion, and especially Arab opinion, was beginning a dangerous shift. Unless the war could be ended promptly, the Coalition could unravel. President Bush, Secretary of Defense Dick Cheney, Joint Chiefs Chair Colin Powell, and General Schwarzkopf knew that they had to be ready for ground action soon.

ON THE
HOME FRONT

The American public followed closely the invasion of Kuwait, the buildup of forces, and the launching of the air war. Through television, newspapers, newsmagazines, and in countless conversations at lunch counters and bars, at bus stops and in medical waiting rooms, the American people reviewed the issues. While everyone had an opinion, for a while facts were scarce. But as the media continued its flow—some of it opinionated and biased, some channeled through close control by military press conferences and media pools in Saudi Arabia, and some striving to convey just the facts—opinion began to be backed up by information.

The Vietnam War had been labeled "the first televised war," the first war "brought into the living room." But those televised reports had been filtered through American networks and were not in real time. In the Gulf War, events were reported more directly. Americans watched the live daily briefings given by the Coalition military in Saudi Arabia. CNN in particular became a presence in millions of homes. The press reported that pizza sales picked up as Americans ate dinner in front of their television sets.

As American troops began to fly into Saudi Arabia, families bedecked their front yards with yellow ribbons tied around trees, shrubs, and even potted plants. Derived from an old popular song, "Tie a Yellow Ribbon 'Round the Old Oak Tree," the symbol was poignant. The ribbon meant that loved ones remembered those far away. The symbol was neutral in a way. Whether one favored the war or had reservations about it, everyone could agree they wanted the troops home safely.

That symbol and others—candlelight vigils, prayer meetings, and the show of American flags—showed that a new sentiment had spread in public opinion, very different from that during the Vietnam

U.S. troops were welcomed home with parades and yellow ribbon displays, including this huge overhead ribbon in San Diego, California. *(DOD Defense Information Center, March ARB, California)*

War. While Americans might have reservations about the war and its conduct, they seemed to be coming together on support of the troops themselves.

As the tension mounted in the Persian Gulf, President Bush's approval rating began to climb. Immediately after the invasion of Kuwait by Iraq, Bush's rating climbed 20 percent as he began to send over troops. By the end of the war, it would top 90 percent in the polls.

A question of timing about public opinion haunted the president and his advisers. Schwarzkopf knew that American mothers and fathers would grow impatient if their sons and daughters had to sit in the sweltering heat of Saudi Arabia for months and years with no prospect of a return. While support was strong, it could fade if no action were taken.

Such considerations fed into the decision by Bush to wait until after the November congressional elections and then to begin the process of readying the public for pushing back the "line in the sand" he had already drawn to defend the Saudi border. As he did so, with his mixed signals, American opinion reflected confusion. The president's public opinion polls slipped again, back to the level before the invasion. Some felt he was moving too fast; others felt he was moving too slowly.

In November, large antiwar demonstrations began to occur throughout the United States. But the demonstrations carried a different tone than the strident antiwar demonstrations of the Vietnam era. Clerics,

During the Desert Shield buildup, Coalition troops set up encampments behind protective sand embankments scraped out of the desert floor. *(DOD Defense Information Center, March ARB, California)*

middle-aged homemakers, and professionals joined young people, asking new sorts of questions. However, unlike some earlier conflicts and
police actions, this one seemed very justified to many.

Word of Iraqi atrocities leaked out. Some of the stories that seemed
to catch public attention were not the gruesome and horrible tales
of rape, murder, and looting but more unique episodes that touched
public sensitivities. When Iraqis threw hundreds of civilians out of
the Kuwait City hospital to make way for their own wounded, the
American media focused on stories that several premature babies had
been taken off life-support incubators and the equipment shipped back
to Iraq. Iraqi soldiers released all the animals from the Kuwaiti zoo,
shooting some of the more edible ones and letting the others wander
until they starved. An elephant wandering the streets and begging gen-
tly with its trunk and a zebra fed for a few days by a sympathetic Iraqi
family caught the public imagination.

Saddam Hussein may have misjudged the effect of his actions in
many ways. Western civilians resident in Iraq were held, and Hussein,
announced they would serve as "human shields" to prevent air attacks

Entertainers Bob Hope and Ann Jillian perform for military personnel in
Saudi Arabia during the USO Christmas tour and prior to launching Operation
Desert Storm. Hope had entertained U.S. forces abroad ever since World
War II. *(Defense Imagery)*

on his facilities. Hussein worked to make propaganda, visiting one camp where hostages were held. On television he introduced a seven-year-old British boy, Stuart Lockwood, indicating that the boy and his family would be safe as long as the West did not attack. The boy, obviously uncomfortable, stood rigidly at attention. Audiences around the world were stunned. Later, on another visit to a hostage camp, a British woman asked him, in front of the cameras, why he thought that he should hold children when they had no understanding of the issues. He was at a loss for words.

When British prime minister Margaret Thatcher accused him of "hiding behind women's skirts," the blow to Arab manhood apparently struck home. On August 28, Hussein announced that all women and children were free to leave. Even so, he sent the male hostages to "vital installations" and arrested more. By the start of October, there were more than 600 hostages at strategic sites, including 260 British, 103 Americans, 141 Japanese, 80 French, and 77 Germans. All had been resident or visiting in Iraq before the war.

Criticism of hostage-holding came not only from the American public and press but from the Arab world as well. Austrian president Kurt Waldheim had visited Baghdad and secured the release of 140 Austrian hostages on August 25. African-American leader Jesse Jackson visited shortly thereafter and returned with four older and ill American male hostages, joining some on a plane with women and children. With mixed propaganda effect, other foreign visitors, including Muhammad Ali, the American former heavyweight boxer and a Muslim, and politicians from Europe, were able to secure the release of a few hostages.

On November 18, Hussein announced that he would release all hostages before Christmas. The gesture, after two months, appeared to win his cause very few supporters in American living rooms. The United Nations passed its resolution demanding that Hussein withdraw his forces by January 15, 1991, or face possible military action.

American opinion polls in early December showed a decidedly split opinion. According to one survey, 45 percent agreed the United States should go to war if the Iraqis did not withdraw. But Bush and his advisers worried about another figure. The same poll showed that 48 percent believed that the Coalition should wait longer, to see if the sanctions on exports from and imports to Iraq had an effect. Some analyses of the polls tried to find out if the divisions related to gender, ethnicity, or other factors. Some reported that men tended to favor action more than did women. One survey showed that 73 percent of women opposed a war to liberate Kuwait. Some thought it was less opposition to war itself or a demand for diplomacy than opposition to the Kuwait regime that did not permit women to vote.

Black and white Americans seemed to have a different opinion mix, although both groups were split. In August, a poll showed that 74 per-

A JUST WAR?

Thinkers on international law since St. Augustine (354–430) and St. Thomas Aquinas (1225–74) have developed seven principles or considerations to determine whether a war is "just" or legitimate. Those in favor and those against the war in the Persian Gulf have debated each of the principles.

1. A just war must be authorized by a legitimate authority.

    Proponents: Both the United Nations and the United States Congress approved the war.

    Opponents: The Bush administration had to pressure UN Security Council members to pass Resolution 678. The vote in the U.S. Senate was close, showing strong opposition to the war.

2. A just war can only be fought if it is started with right intentions, such as to redress a wrong.

    Proponents: The war goal was to redress the Iraqi invasion of Kuwait.

    Opponents: The real motive was American interest in the oil resources of Kuwait.

3. A war cannot be justified if its chances of success are low and it appears that it will drag on for an extended period.

    Proponents: The Coalition mounted a huge army, air force, and navy from 34 nations. The war lasted only 100 hours, proof that chance of success was reasonable.

    Opponents: The Iraqi army was well-equipped and extremely large. The fact that Coalition military leaders had to assemble 400,000 troops proves how risky the war was.

4. The damage of the war must be proportional to the injury suffered.

cent of whites approved Bush's decision to send U.S. troops to the gulf, while only 41 percent of blacks agreed. Perhaps the difference was due to a memory of Vietnam, when a disproportionate number of troops in the front lines were black. In the Persian Gulf War, as it turned out, most casualties would be pilots, mostly middle-class whites.

The rallies across the United States continued to reflect a mixed view. Some signs and bumper stickers read: "Bring the Troops Home."

Proponents: Expelling Iraq from Kuwait was exactly in proportion to the injury of the Iraqi invasion of Kuwait.

Opponents: The massive destruction of facilities in Iraq was out of proportion to the damage Iraq imposed on Kuwait. The war left billions of dollars of damage to the oil fields and the environment.

5. A just war should be waged only as a last resort.

Proponents: Saddam Hussein was given ample warning to pull forces out of Kuwait or face attack. He refused.

Opponents: U.S. Ambassador April Glaspie misled Hussein by failing to tell him the United States would oppose an invasion of Kuwait by force. Negotiation should have continued.

6. The real reason for the war should show right intent and should be the stated reason.

Proponents: The real and stated reason was the liberation of Kuwait from its invasion by Iraq.

Opponents: The United States had special interests in the Kuwait oil fields and feared Iraqi domination of the oil production of the world.

7. The goal of a just war should be to reestablish peace. The peace established after the war should be better than the peace that would exist if the war were not fought.

Proponents: Kuwait was liberated and peace established quickly, without an extended invasion of Iraq itself.

Opponents: Peace left severe problems. Western troops stationed in Saudi Arabia, regarded by Muslims as a holy land, enraged radical Islamic leaders. Iraq continued to represent a threat to peace in the region. Hussein brutally suppressed Shiite Arabs in the south of his own country. They had been encouraged to rebel by the Coalition attack on Iraq.

Others read: "Nuke Iraq." Between were milder ones, urging peace and pressure. Demonstrators on both sides of the issue often seemed to agree that free discussion was crucial, and often those who remembered antiwar demonstrations from the Vietnam days remarked on the change. Over and over, demonstrators on both sides of the issue could agree: They supported the troops and wanted them home safe. Rallies included groups carrying signs for other causes such as gay rights and nuclear disarmament, along with support for the troops and their families. The quality and tone of the demonstrations was completely different from those two decades earlier.

The public continued to support servicemen and -women in new ways. Thousands of bars and saloons turned their televisions from the sports channels to CNN. Christmas cards and presents were mailed to "Any U.S. Soldier," Saudi Arabia. Later, Valentine cards with the same kind of address flooded the mailbags to Saudi Arabia. Blood donations increased, yellow ribbons proliferated, and here and there, someone found an Iraqi flag to burn. Despite the flood of information coming from the television, rumors and misinformation spread. Many feared that Iraq would support a terror attack in the

Lt. Gen. Khalid bin Sultan bin Abdul Aziz, commander of the Joint Forces in Saudi Arabia, escorts Secretary of Defense Richard Cheney upon his arrival for a meeting to discuss the Coalition's plans for Operation Desert Storm. *(Defense Imagery)*

THE REPUBLICAN GUARD

As American viewers watched the news, they learned of the Iraqi Republican Guard. Hussein moved 30,000 members of this elite force to the border with Kuwait in July 1990. General Schwarzkopf regarded the destruction of the Republican Guard as a major war objective. During the air campaign that began on January 16, 1991, Coalition aircraft especially targeted Republican Guard positions, seeking to destroy their heavy weapons and tanks.

During Desert Storm, U.S. and British troops encountered more than 90,000 Republican Guard troops north of Kuwait. Three armored divisions of the Republican Guard, the Tawalkana, Medina, and the Hammurabi Divisions, put up stiff resistance on February 25 through February 27. Despite reports that they fought well, their Soviet tanks were outclassed by heavier M1 American tanks, supported by Warthog aircraft and F-16 fighters. An estimated 700 Republican Guard tanks were destroyed in clashes near the end of the war.

United States, perhaps bombing a Disney theme park or blowing up the Alaska oil pipeline.

After the January 15 deadline by the United Nations had been announced, further public opinion polls in the United States continued to show mixed opinions. Remembering Vietnam, and still concerned about casualties in a foreign war, the public provided some interesting results for the analysts. In one early January poll, 63 percent supported military action in Iraq. But when confronted with how they would support a war with 1,000 Americans killed, the support dropped to 44 percent and to only 35 percent if the figure suggested were 10,000. Clearly, Americans would support action, but that support could easily wither when faced with returning body bags.

Powell and Cheney asked Schwarzkopf for an estimate of what the war would cost in casualties. Giving his best guess of a worst case on December 19, Schwarzkopf suggested there might be 20,000 casualties, with 7,000 killed in an action to eject Iraq from Kuwait. Although the figure was not immediately made public, outside military experts, looking at the same factors, suggested unofficial estimates from a few hundred up to 15,000. The media picked up on such estimates and soon suggested that the coming war might be a "bloodbath."

Fears of poison gas and biological and nuclear weapons haunted such discussions.

Some experts opposed a ground war, suggesting that an air campaign would hold Coalition casualties to a minimum. But Schwarzkopf and his advisers insisted that there was no way to dislodge the Iraqis without a ground assault. As Powell noted, an air campaign alone would leave the decision about withdrawal in Hussein's hands. He would have to decide how much punishment was enough. Again, timing would be crucial. Even if the Coalition were willing to back up the air campaign with a ground assault, the members' patience could wear thin, and leaders might decide to push the assault too early.

But CENTCOM had a plan ready, and early in February 1990 General Schwarzkopf and his staff prepared to push the Iraqis out of Kuwait.

DESERT STORM
BEGINS

The battle plan that General Schwarzkopf and CENTCOM had developed in detail followed the established AirLand Battle doctrine that had been standard operating procedure for the U.S. Defense Department since 1983. Applying lessons from Vietnam and reflecting planning for a ground war in Europe against Soviet forces, the AirLand doctrine called for penetrating behind enemy lines with air attacks that cut off supplies and communications, isolating the enemy's troops at the front line. Then armored units would make deep pushes ahead with artillery, naval, and air bombardment on specific targets, throwing the enemy off guard.

By dividing the enemy forces into sections and cutting the enemy off from its central command and control, allied forces could then destroy the sections. The planning for a launch in February into Kuwait and Iraq was thrown off, however, when the Iraqis suddenly invaded Saudi Arabia on January 29. Nearly a month before the Coalition planned attack to liberate Kuwait, the enemy took the initiative.

On January 29, elements of the Iraqi Fifth Armored Division swept into the Saudi resort town of Ras al-Khafji, a few miles south of the Kuwaiti-Saudi border on the Persian Gulf. A U.S. Marine reconnaissance group provided the only defense for the deserted town. As the marines fell back, the Iraqi raid with heavy Russian-built tanks against lighter American forces at first appeared like a Coalition disaster. At the same time, brigade-sized Iraqi units attacked along two other lines into Saudi Arabia, to the west of Khafji.

U.S. Marines of the First Light Armored Infantry Battalion called in artillery and close air support from helicopters and Warthog A-10 aircraft. The light infantry battalion had no heavy armor, even though it had antitank weapons. Unfortunately, during these engagements, 11

Americans were killed by friendly fire. One Warthog fired a missile that hit an American light attack vehicle, killing seven inside. During the engagement, another four soldiers were killed by friendly ground fire.

Meanwhile, two six-person marine teams undetected by the Iraqis hid inside buildings in Khafji. These marines provided valuable intelligence details about the types of tanks and the numbers of troops the enemy had, information that helped in planning the counterattack. Joint Arab forces, including Saudi National Guard and tanks from Qatar, backed by marines, conducted the counterattack. The Coalition Arab forces suffered 10 dead and 45 wounded in the battle. The battle finally turned in favor of the Coalition, with the destruction of 33 Iraqi tanks and 29 Iraqi armored personnel carriers. By February 1, the Iraqis had pulled back from Ras al-Khafji and from the other points to the west where they had penetrated.

The Coalition learned a hard lesson from this first encounter: the need to be extremely careful of friendly fire accidents. However, it felt encouraged that a combination of light marine forces, air attack, and joint Arab armored forces stood up against one of the strongest Iraqi units and drove them back. Although only a minor skirmish, the battle was a Coalition victory.

The U.S. Marine Corps employed the M1A1 Abrams main battle tank as they moved into Kuwait in the ground phase of Operation Desert Storm. (*Defense Imagery*)

Gen. Colin Powell briefs President Bush, Secretaries Baker and Cheney, and others on February 24, 1991, the first day of the ground phase of Operation Desert Storm. *(George Bush Presidential Library)*

Coalition forces launched the long-awaited massive attack on Sunday morning February 24. There were two relatively distinct parts of the main attack. U.S. Marines and joint Arab forces advanced directly into Kuwait, facing strong fortifications and mixed resistance. Even so, they would meet their objective of taking Kuwait City more rapidly than planned.

Further to the west, on the left flank, French, British, and American forces organized into two corps. XVIII Corps moved on the far west, or outer flank, and VII Corps advanced just west of the Iraqi-Kuwait border. These two corps faced very weak fortifications and troops that offered practically no opposition to the first advances. The fast moving attack of XVIII Corps, which included two famous U.S. paratrooper divisions, the Eighty-second and the 101st, went rapidly with little opposition during the first three days. But VII Corps moved ahead more methodically.

The Coalition ground forces were estimated at 575,000 troops, and altogether the Coalition had about 3,700 tanks and 1,500 artillery pieces. The Iraqis had a force estimated after the air bombardment of about 220,000 troops, about 1,700 tanks, and 1,000 artillery pieces. A combination of desertion, casualties, and air bombardment had resulted in a two-to-one advantage for the Coalition. Despite such a balance, given the fact that defense almost always requires less force than offense, the chances of the Coalition's success were not at all certain.

The Iraqis had used their six months in Kuwait to construct defensive lines, including minefields, bunkers, sand berms, and oil-filled trenches that could be ignited if Coalition forces tried to cross. Despite the bombardment, they were dug in, with tanks and artillery often cleverly concealed.

The Coalition forces used distraction and deception. The U.S. Navy and the U.S. Marines conducted maneuvers off the shore of Kuwait, drawing Iraqi attention to the wrong place by threatening an amphibious landing that never took place. A light Coalition force maneuvered for several days near the Kuwait/Saudi frontier, creating the false impression of a major buildup there. Both of these feints helped confuse the enemy. On February 22 and 23, before the main attack, commandos and marines moved quietly into Iraq ahead of the main force. Black Hawk helicopters took in troops before the official invasion began, some men carrying heavy 40-pound sacks of explosives and other equipment. Several of these units engaged in intensive firefights with Iraqi units. Close air support called in by radio aided the ground troops in these small battles.

On Sunday morning, February 24, 1990, the strong French and American forces in XVIII Corps, including airborne and armored troops, swung around in their flanking attack. At the same time, VII Corps, including the U.S. Twenty-fourth Infantry Division, had the job of penetrating far into Iraq to attack Iraqi divisions in the rear. To prepare these two flanking groups, the Coalition had to move 200,000 troops with all their equipment as much as 300 miles to the west in secret.

The quiet move of forces to the west in preparation for the attack came in what Schwarzkopf began to call the "Hail Mary" maneuver. He named the strategy after a football play in which a quarterback throws a pass in the general direction of one corner of the end zone, hoping one of his receivers will be there. Newsmen picked up the term and used it to describe the troops' veering far into the desert to get around Iraqi main defense lines.

Iraqi military equipment, although relatively modern, was poorly maintained, as Coalition troops learned when they found weapons such as this abandoned Iraqi antiaircraft gun on the beach in Kuwait City after reclaiming the city. *(Defense Imagery)*

The move worked, almost without a hitch. Unfortunately, a few days before the battle, a newsmagazine presented such a plan as a possible alternative. For a moment, Schwarzkopf thought security had been breached, but his advisers soon pointed out that with the mass of alternatives being suggested by the media, Iraq had no reason to believe this one above any other.

VII Corps had the job of moving ahead on the left flank, but not as far west as XVIII Corps, to an objective code-named "Collins," a 10-mile wide oval of gravel desert to the west of the main location of the Iraqi Republican Guard. There, Gen. Fred Franks was to regroup and prepare to launch his forces at the Republican Guard. However, after the first night of the attack, it was clear that VII Corps had moved only a few miles into Iraq, not very far toward its objective.

Schwarzkopf later recalled in his autobiography, *It Doesn't Take a Hero,* that he called Gen. John Yeosock, who had insisted on commanding his troops within VII Corps, despite returning from major surgery two days before G ("go")-Day. "Did VII Corps stop for the night?" asked Schwarzkopf. "Look," he said, "I don't want them to do anything stupid, but they haven't had a shot fired at them as far as I know. They seem to be just sitting around. What's going on?" It appeared that Schwarzkopf was ready to launch into one of his famous rages.

Yeosock called back in a few hours. He explained that Franks was sticking with the original schedule. He had passed the initial barriers, had reorganized his forces, and would be ready to attack the Republican Guard the next day. Schwarzkopf was satisfied. The plan could still work, because intelligence showed that the Republican Guard still held its position to the north of Kuwait. Yet to the west of VII Corps, the wide-flanking group of XVIII Corps had to slow down, as Schwarzkopf did not want them to encounter the Republican Guard by themselves. Watching the faster advance in some places and the slower, more methodical advance in others, Schwarzkopf likened it to trying to drive a wagon pulled by a team made up of racehorses and mules.

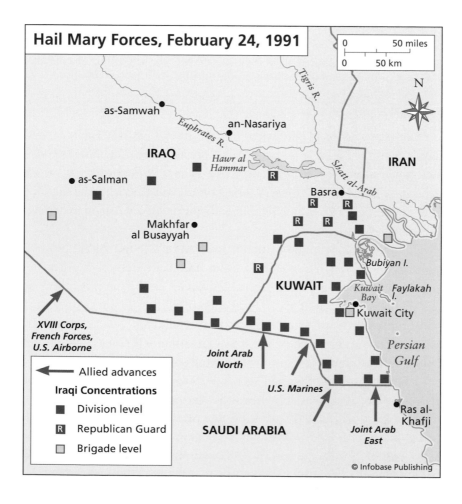

Hail Mary Forces, February 24, 1991

© Infobase Publishing

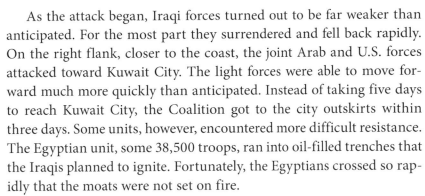

As the attack began, Iraqi forces turned out to be far weaker than anticipated. For the most part they surrendered and fell back rapidly. On the right flank, closer to the coast, the joint Arab and U.S. forces attacked toward Kuwait City. The light forces were able to move forward much more quickly than anticipated. Instead of taking five days to reach Kuwait City, the Coalition got to the city outskirts within three days. Some units, however, encountered more difficult resistance. The Egyptian unit, some 38,500 troops, ran into oil-filled trenches that the Iraqis planned to ignite. Fortunately, the Egyptians crossed so rapidly that the moats were not set on fire.

The allied forces in the Coalition worked well together. French paratroopers in XVIII Corps moved in the first day and a half into as-Salman, far out to the west in the Iraqi desert, and then set up a defensive position to repel a possible counterattack around and behind the advancing Coalition forces. The only French casualties occurred when the paratroopers accidentally detonated unexploded antipersonnel devices from American cluster bombs. The explosives killed two paratroopers and wounded 25 others.

Mass surrenders of Iraqi troops began immediately. By Tuesday, about 50 hours after the operation began, the Coalition stopped counting prisoners of war (POWs) at 30,000. Often large numbers of Iraqi soldiers surrendered to far smaller units. Many of the prisoners were hungry, sick, and even thirsty, begging for water. At first, U.S. troops loaded prisoners into trucks for transport to the rear but soon ran out of vehicles. Finally, American soldiers simply took the prisoners' weapons, lined them up, pointed south, and told them "March that way." Further back, checkpoints rounded up the prisoners. As reports of casualties came in, Coalition officers had trouble believing them. In one report from the advancing left flank, Gen. Gary Luck reported he had 3,200 prisoners and was still counting. The total casualties suffered by his forces was only one wounded.

In the push directly into Kuwait, marines fought off three Iraqi counterattacks, destroyed scores of Iraqi tanks, and took huge numbers of prisoners, all in the first day. These marines reported one dead and 18 wounded. Working with General Khalid of Saudi Arabia, Schwarzkopf ordered the Egyptian force on that front to move ahead of schedule, so they could catch up for the liberation of Kuwait City. Like VII Corps, the Egyptian forces tended to move methodically, initially sticking to their schedule.

A crucial part of the advance in the first two days was close air support. In most instances where Coalition planes were shot down, U.S. helicopters would pick up the fliers, while Warthogs shot up any enemy forces attempting to capture the grounded crew.

After seven marines were killed by friendly fire from an aircraft at Khafji, they took special measures to prevent further such tragedies. Fluorescent orange sheets on top of armored personnel carriers and special armbands that emitted infrared signals warned air crews that potential targets were Coalition. The other four marines killed by friendly fire at Khafji were victims of ground fire. Even with added caution, another 20 U.S. soldiers died from friendly ground fire and four more from Coalition air strikes.

The air war against the Iraqi infrastructure had cut supplies to Iraqi troops in Kuwait by 90 percent, from 20,000 tons per day to about 2,000 tons per day. As the ground war got under way, Coalition aircraft used jellied gasoline (napalm) to ignite oil that the Iraqis had let into tank trap trenches at the border, and bombs destroyed networks of pipelines

Coalition troops examine a Soviet-built Iraqi T-55 main battle tank destroyed by the French forces during Operation Desert Storm. *(Defense Imagery)*

WOMEN IN THE U.S. MILITARY

The Gulf War was the first in which American women had officially participated in combat, although during earlier wars numerous women, disguised as men, had served surreptitiously in combat roles, and in earlier wars women filled many support positions. Roughly 6 to 7 percent of U.S. troops in the Gulf War were women: 30,000 army, 4,000 air force, 4,700 navy, and 1,200 marines. Women served as air traffic controllers, clerks, cooks, firefighters, intelligence officers, mechanics, security guards, truck drivers, helicopter pilots, and administrators. The total U.S. ground forces reached about 575,000, with women representing nearly 40,000 of that number.

In field camps, enlisted women had their own tents and latrines, but without much privacy. Nevertheless, "the females," as they were called, managed under the conditions. The women did their part to make sure they did not get special treatment, refusing to let the men carry their gear or similar things.

Of the 148 American troops killed in action, four were women. In addition, 16 women were wounded in action and two were taken prisoner. None of the female casualties occurred in frontline, direct action;

(continues)

Female U.S. military personnel take part in an informal briefing on the eve of their deployment to Operation Desert Shield, the preparatory phase for what would become Operation Desert Storm. *(Defense Imagery)*

(continued)

they were the result of mines, Scud attacks, or helicopter crashes. After the Persian Gulf War, the Defense Department decided to allow female pilots to fly combat missions.

Surprisingly, the conservative United Arab Emirates (UAE) started training women soldiers after seeing the American women's performance. Wearing special uniforms with head coverings that conformed to Muslim customs, female UAE soldiers later went through a five-month training session under American women instructors. Arab officers were so impressed with their performance in training that they decided to include them in future noncombatant roles and to consider such roles as missile operators or pilots.

and pumps the Iraqis had set up to feed oil to the tank trap system. B-52 heavy bombers and helicopter gunships swept over defensive lines, softening them for the armored advances. A-10 Warthog ground attack aircraft crews spent much of the first two days waiting on the ground, ready in case they were needed. They could hit almost anywhere in the battlefield within 10 to 20 minutes. But for the most part, the ground forces moved so swiftly that once they started on February 24, there were few calls for air support from the Warthog tank-busters.

In the "fog of war," the view of soldiers on the ground varied greatly from one engagement to another. While most of the Coalition attack to liberate Kuwait was made by armored forces in tanks and light armored vehicles, there were a few infantry actions. When the invasion began at 4:00 A.M. on February 24, some 2,700 marines were already 22 miles into Iraq, ready to head up to take the al-Jaber airfield. These troops explored minefields by hand, marking them out with flags or shooting line charges to open paths through others. As these troops advanced toward the second line of barriers that they sought to destroy, the Iraqis fired artillery. The marines then called in air strikes, and fighter/attack aircraft would come in to take out the artillery battery.

Meanwhile, French armored troops compared their speed to an old-fashioned cavalry charge or to the beginning of a Grand Prix auto race. Out on the left flank, French and U.S. helicopters moved forward with the armor, rapidly getting to their position at as-Salman and protecting VII Corps for the breakthrough in the center of the line.

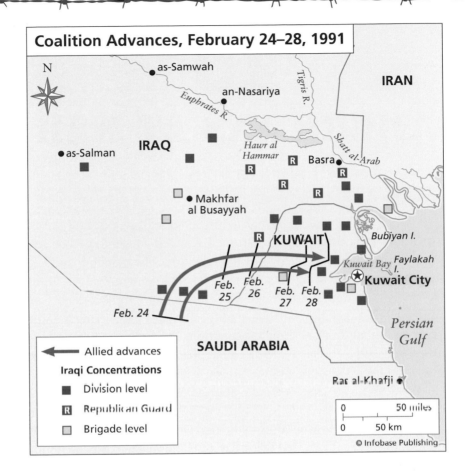

Coalition Advances, February 24–28, 1991

N

as-Samwah

IRAN

Euphrates R.

an-Nasariya

Tigris R.

as-Salman

IRAQ

Hawr al Hammar

R Basra

Shatt al-Arab

R

R

R

R

R

R

Makhfar al Busayyah

R KUWAIT

Bubiyan I.

Kuwait Bay *Faylakah I.*

⬟ **Kuwait City**

Feb. 25   Feb. 26   Feb. 27   Feb. 28

Feb. 24

Persian Gulf

SAUDI ARABIA

Ras al-Khafji

← Allied advances

Iraqi Concentrations

■ Division level

R Republican Guard

☐ Brigade level

0   50 miles

0   50 km

© Infobase Publishing

Back in Kuwait, Syrian forces in the Coalition were equipped with Soviet tanks, so in order to avoid incidents of friendly fire, commanders maintained wide separation between the Syrian forces and other Coalition groups in American and British armor. Since the Iraqis also had Soviet armor, it would be all too easy to mistake a friendly Syrian tank for an enemy Iraqi one.

Although joint Arab forces reached the outskirts of Kuwait City by 5 P.M. local time on Tuesday, February 26, the push to destroy the Republican Guard forces and to drive the Iraqis back from southern Iraq would be more difficult. The two U.S. airborne divisions from the far left joined the five divisions of VII Corps. The flanking movement had been successful, and these joint forces now turned east to hit the Republican Guard and other Iraqi troops remaining in northern Kuwait and in Iraq south of the city of Basra. To use Schwarzkopf's analogy, the mules and the racehorses were now ready to pull together.

AMERICANS AT WAR

February 26-28

The Coalition's original plan assumed a much longer war, but the massive Iraqi surrenders changed the schedule. The bombing and the fear of the overwhelming Coalition forces had demoralized the Iraqi troops. In addition, many tough veterans of the long Iraq-Iran war confessed that they did not believe in the cause of conquering Kuwait or in taking on the American-led coalition. Outgunned and outnumbered in most positions, they either surrendered or tried to retreat back into Iraq, heading north and west toward Baghdad. In one sense, the Coalition victories depended on a failure of enemy morale as much as on equipment and tactics.

In any case, the Coalition's strategy worked brilliantly. On the evening of February 26, the third day of the war, the basic outflanking strategy had already succeeded. The six divisions (Egypt, Syrian, Saudi/Kuwait, two U.S. Marine divisions, and one joint Arab division) attacking in the south had reached Kuwait City.

In the west, the U.S. 82nd and 101st Airborne Divisions that came in from the far-left flank operation of XVIII Corps reinforced the five divisions of the VII Corps that had broken through west of the Kuwait-Iraq border. This massive force then turned to the right to attack the remaining 15 divisions of Iraqi troops, including the Republican Guard, to the north of Kuwait City.

General Schwarzkopf admitted that he had been too harsh in judging the slow progress of VII Corps, later remarking that it was easy to lose sight of battle conditions when he was sitting in a war room deep underground, listening to reports come in. Although his memoirs report his cool judgment on this issue, his reputation for "chewing out" officers had earned him the nickname "Stormin' Norman." No doubt those forces that held back had seen a display of his temper. Yet in some cases, conditions called for the kind of deliberate forward motion ordered by the commanders on the scene. VII Corps moved carefully up the center, preserving its lines of communication and defending against possible counterattacks.

The 24th Infantry Division, from VII Corps, began to move on Tuesday, February 26, toward the Euphrates River to cut off Iraqi retreat. During this 50-mile push, the Twenty-fourth encountered stiff Iraqi resistance but destroyed hundreds of Iraqi tanks and other vehicles in night fighting. The 24th Division advanced so fast that its fuel-supply trucks could not keep up. It halted at midnight, to allow the fuel trucks to catch up and to get a start again early on February 27.

By 6:00 A.M. Wednesday, February 27, the 24th Infantry Division was in position to attack the Jalibah Air Base, and by 10:00 A.M. the troops took their objective. In that battle, the division's 2nd Brigade destroyed a tank battalion, 80 antiaircraft guns, 20 Iraqi airplanes, and the fuel and ammunition stocks at the base. The airbase had been a threat because of its communication equipment. As the U.S. tanks

U.S. Marines ride into Kuwait International Airport after the retreat of Iraqi forces. *(DOD Defense Information Center)*

A U.S. Marine uses a field radio following the withdrawal of Iraqi troops during Operation Desert Storm. *(DOD Defense Information Center, March ARB, California)*

rolled in at high speed, they destroyed helicopters, radar dishes, trucks, and other equipment. Later, American officers learned that the Iraqis had assumed that the attack on the airbase signaled a Coalition plan to go on to take Baghdad, helping to account for sudden movement from defensive positions of the Republican Guard.

As the Republican Guard tanks moved out from their berm-protected emplacements, Warthogs and fighter-attack aircraft could catch them in the open. Even with the smoke from oil field fires and the burning vehicles, aircraft and tanks could find their targets with infrared heat detection equipment. The difficulty with such methods, however, was that unless a vehicle could be visually identified, it might turn out to be friendly.

Meanwhile, in the center, the attack of VII Corps had also proceeded on Tuesday, February 26, and Wednesday, February 27. As Coalition forces came into the outskirts of Kuwait City from the south and southwest, and as Coalition heavy units of VII Corps moved in from the west, Iraqi units began to flee in disorder to the north.

Arranged in an arc around the west and north of Kuwait, six divisions of the Republican Guard stood as a barrier to the advancing VII

Corps armor. Each of the Republican Guard divisions had a name drawn from ancient Babylonian history. Directly in the path of the advancing VII Corps were the Tawalkana, Medina, and Nebuchadnezzar Divisions. Behind and to the north, between the northern border of Kuwait and the Iraqi city of Basra, were the Al-Faw, Adnan, and Hammurabi Divisions.

The Eagle Troop of the U.S. 2nd Armored Cavalry Unit consisted of less than 200 soldiers with nine large M1 tanks and 14 Bradley fighting vehicles. The Eagle Troop encountered parts of the Tawalkana Division on the afternoon of Tuesday, February 26. In a battle named "73 Easting," because of the map coordinates, this small force destroyed 28 Iraqi tanks and 16 armored personnel carriers, while taking no losses on their own.

On the morning of Wednesday, February 27, in the Battle of Medina Ridge, the 2nd Brigade of the U.S. 1st Armored Division with

Defeat of the Republican Guard, February 26–28, 1991

© Infobase Publishing

166 M1 tanks engaged a brigade of the Medina Division. The Americans started firing at 3,000 meters (almost two miles), moving forward as they fired. Altogether, within an hour the M1s destroyed 61 Iraqi tanks and 34 armored personnel carriers. With support from Warthogs and fighter aircraft, they destroyed another 200 armored Iraqi vehicles. The enemy hit two U.S. Bradleys, resulting in one American dead and several wounded.

The bare statistics do not convey the heat of battle, in which American tank and Bradley personnel searched out the enemy through dust, smoke, and early morning darkness. Before firing, each commander tried to be sure that the target in front was enemy, not friendly. Later investigation showed that of five Bradley vehicles hit in the engagement of Alpha Troop with elements of the Tawalkana Division, three had been hit by friendly fire. Two men were killed, and Alpha Troop received many decorations, the most for any company-sized unit in the war.

When American vehicles were hit, others came to their aid, shielding them from further fire. Gunners and drivers then rushed to pull the wounded from the burning machines, trying to get them out before their own ammunition blew up. For nearly all of the Americans, it was the first military action they had seen, and the severe wounds and death of comrades in the rush of battle was a shock that took a while to register. As medics came up to help, they had to work in the dark and in the midst of confusing fire, setting up an aid station to treat the wounded within range of enemy artillery.

The Iraqis who retreated from Kuwait City on Tuesday, February 26 faced another kind of horror. Tens of thousands of soldiers loaded into trucks and stolen civilian cars, driving out of the city and creating a huge traffic jam more than a mile long. Many carried looted belongings, ranging from clothes and jewelry through furniture and even light fixtures. The straight road toward Basra, Iraq, turns slightly uphill outside Kuwait City near Mitla Pass. Coalition aircraft soon detected the column and dropped mines in front and behind the line of vehicles to block movement and then directed heavy fire against the lead vehicles on the uphill slope. Attacking aircraft had to wait in line for their turn to fire on the stalled convoy.

On the evening of February 26, the 2nd Armored Division also poured in tank fire. Soon the whole line was completely wrecked and burning. More than 2,000 vehicles were destroyed along the Mitla Pass road. Initial reports indicated that many Iraqis died on this stretch of road, but later the 2nd Armored Division troops discovered that most Iraqis had fled into the desert on foot, leaving the burning vehicles behind. Even so, the grotesque burned corpses of those caught in the vehicles shocked Coalition observers when they came on the wreckage later.

Photos from the air and later photos on the ground soon earned the caption "highway of death." The descriptions in the press suggested it was comparable to a turkey shoot (in which domestic turkeys are slaughtered by shotgun) or shooting fish in a barrel. The sudden shocked concern in the media contributed to public and political pressure to bring a quick end to the conflict. From a military point of view, however, the best time to attack is when the enemy is in a disorganized retreat. The reality of war was difficult to understand when viewed through civilian eyes, yet in this instance, even some hardened war veterans found the carnage disturbing.

As the Iraqis retreated, they not only left their own and stolen vehicles burning behind them, but they also set on fire about 600 of

The trail of destroyed vehicles, including trucks and buses, on the so-called highway of death shocked even hardened veterans. *(DOD Defense Information Center, March ARB, California)*

OIL POLLUTION AS A WEAPON

Iraqi forces set on fire about 600 oil wells in Kuwait and released more than 125 million gallons of oil into the Persian Gulf. In an era of increased awareness of the fragility of the Earth's environment, such measures seemed wanton acts of vandalism. However, the Iraqis had turned crude oil into a potent military and economic weapon.

The bill for the oil field repair work was staggering. The San Francisco–based Bechtel Group agreed to an initial cost of repairs of $150 million, with future costs of the oil field repairs expected to approach $6 billion.

The oil released into the gulf was nearly 10 times the amount in the 1989 *Exxon Valdez* tanker spill in Alaskan waters. Estimates of the cleanup cost of the Persian Gulf waters ran more than $5 billion. Teams from Japan, Norway, and the United States participated in the work.

The immediate problem was to snuff out the 600 oil well fires. Several American companies, including the "Red" Adair team (named after its American leader, famed for putting out oil well fires), brought their experience to the task. Using fire shields, foam, and cooling water, workers would approach a flaming well head to place dynamite. When detonated, the blast would literally blow out the fire, momentarily cutting off the air supply. Then the teams installed a new well head that contained a massive faucetlike valve. They would then turn off the flow of gas and oil and later connect new pipes to the valve.

Kuwait's 1,000 oil wells. The clouds of smoke from the burning wells obscured the sky, limiting Coalition air power in the last days of the war. One of Hussein's objectives had been to reduce Kuwaiti oil production to help drive up the international price of crude oil, and that he had achieved, at least temporarily.

Back in Kuwait City, the Iraqis had also burned office buildings, gutted hospitals of equipment, released all the animals from the zoo to starve or be shot, ruined the water desalination plant, and destroyed oil refineries.

On February 26, Saddam Hussein announced that he would order all troops withdrawn from Kuwait. At the same time, however, he reiterated his claim that Kuwait was a province of Iraq. His wording was

The environmental damage was difficult to estimate. The dark smoke over Kuwait reduced the temperature some 20 degrees, and acid rain, rich in sulfur dioxide, threatened food crops in Kuwait and nearby Saudi Arabia.

As Iraqi forces retreated from Kuwait and southern Iraq, they set oil wells on fire. For some time these fires created a major environmental disaster. *(Defense Imagery)*

ambiguous, suggesting that Kuwait would have an independent government only because he pulled out his troops. Furthermore, he made no indication that Iraq would pay for any part of the damage his forces had brought to Kuwait. Coalition officers in the field and UN officials found the withdrawal order unsatisfactory, especially since Republican Guard units continued to fight, not withdraw.

Later, as the Coalition destroyed and captured more Iraqi divisions, Iraq's foreign minister, Tariq Aziz, announced that Iraq would rescind its annexation of Kuwait, release all prisoners of war, and pay war reparations. All five permanent members of the UN Security Council (the United States, the Russian Federation, the United Kingdom, China, and France) rejected the Iraqi announcement of a cease-fire. First, they

An Iroquois helicopter flies by the battle-damaged control tower at Kuwait International Airport. Much of Kuwait's infrastructure was damaged during the war but it was soon repaired. *(Defense Imagery)*

said, Iraq would have to accept all 12 resolutions the United Nations had passed condemning the Iraqi invasion in the first place.

On February 27, Iraq's ambassador to the United Nations told the Security Council that Iraq would agree to all the resolutions. Furthermore, he said, on that morning, the last Iraqi soldier had left Kuwait, leaving no excuse for further military action.

Powell and Schwarzkopf discussed the exact timing of the cease-fire. Schwarzkopf wanted a few more hours, possibly a day, to complete the destruction of the Republican Guard and other Iraqi units. Although troops were escaping, he needed time to destroy the remaining tanks. After some discussion, President Bush ordered Schwarzkopf to suspend military operations at midnight (Eastern Standard Time in the United States) on February 27, exactly 100 hours after the beginning of Desert Storm.

With the announcement in hand, in the last remaining hours the U.S. Army's 24th Division continued to chase Iraqi units, attacking logistics and ammunition storage bunkers. Even so, one of the remaining Republican Guard units, the Nebuchadnezzar Division, appeared to have escaped the closing net.

The Coalition forces had already penetrated and occupied about 15 percent of Iraq, and they had destroyed between 36 and 40 Iraqi divisions, leaving between three and seven divisions more or less operational. The Coalition had almost, but not quite, achieved the objective of completely wiping out Hussein's powerful army.

Yet the primary objective of the war had been achieved: the removal of Iraqi forces from Kuwait. General Khalid made it clear that Arab members of the Coalition, in particular, had not signed on for an invasion of Iraq or for an attack on Baghdad. And in the United States, no senior official argued for continuing on to "liberate" Iraq or for pushing on toward the capital of the nation.

After the announced cease-fire, on March 1 and 2, escaping remnants of the Hammurabi Division fired on the U.S. 24th Division. In a bitter firefight, the Americans destroyed more than 400 trucks and 187 armored vehicles. Surviving Hammurabi Division troops fled on foot toward Basra.

General Schwarzkopf and an Iraqi general arrive at Safwan to discuss the terms of the Iraqi surrender. *(DOD Defense Information Center, March ARB, California)*

General Schwarzkopf and other U.S. military leaders were glad to see the end of the fighting. A Coalition advance would meet stiffer resistance and higher casualties, and all officers sought to avoid needless loss of life. Interrogators found that Iraqi POWs did not support the cause of invading Kuwait, but defending their homeland was another matter. The United States and the other allies in the Coalition had come through the war with very light casualties, but all that could have changed overnight if they pushed on to the north.

Field commanders signed the formal cease-fire the next Sunday, March 3. Iraqi officers met the Coalition leaders at Safwan, an Iraqi air base less than five miles from the Kuwaiti border. Schwarzkopf intentionally chose the site inside Iraq to demonstrate that it was a meeting of victors with a conquered foe. Schwarzkopf arrived by helicopter. American Bradleys and two M1 tanks escorted the delegation of Iraqis, headed by Gen. Sultan Hashim Ahmad, to the site. They rode in American Humvees.

In a two-hour meeting, the Iraqis agreed to all demands. Details included how to avoid accidental firefights as the two sides disengaged and terms of information exchange about missing soldiers. The Iraqis promised to help identify the land mines that they had planted.

The war was over.

IMMEDIATE AFTERMATH

In the years following the Persian Gulf War, journalists and political pundits debated the wisdom of halting the advance of Coalition forces and not proceeding to Baghdad to conquer Iraq and possibly bring Saddam Hussein before a tribunal for war crimes. But at the time, U.S. policy advisers and Coalition leaders agreed that the job had been done. The UN resolution called upon member states to help use force to expel Iraq from Kuwait. It did not call upon them to support a change of regime in Iraq. Furthermore, the Arab members of the Coalition had explicitly indicated that they would participate only in the liberation of Kuwait. The deployment of troops had reflected that preference, with Arab units going directly into Kuwait, while British, French, and American troops had been used to swing wide through Iraq in the Hail Mary maneuver.

Even so, British and American public opinion polls indicated discontent with the decision not to pursue Hussein. Ninety percent in one British poll thought Hussein should be brought to trial, while in the United States a survey by *Newsweek* showed that 71 percent thought war goals should include toppling Hussein.

President Bush had suggested early in the war that the Iraqi people should force Hussein from power, and in speeches and public statements, Bush often spoke of a "war against Saddam." Even so, U.S. State Department spokespeople several times announced that the United States had no intention of destroying Iraq or challenging its territorial integrity.

It was precisely that desire to maintain Iraq's central authority that concerned many powers other than the United States. In the Middle East, Turkey and Iran did not want to see a powerful Kurdish state. In the northern section of the country, the Kurdish people had a long history of grievances against the regime of Hussein.

On March 6, 1991, President Bush addressed a joint session of Congress to report on Operation Desert Storm and its outcome. *(George Bush Presidential Library)*

In the southern region of the Basra province bordering Iran, Shiite Muslims also sought regional autonomy. But Saudi Arabia and the Gulf States did not want to see a Shiite regime take over some or all of the country.

Even Israel could see the advantage of leaving Saddam Hussein in power. If he were removed, a new dictator might gain respectability and help build up anti-Israeli forces. But with Hussein in power and discredited among other Arabs, at least Iraq would be excluded from regional power politics for a period. Some hoped that perhaps a group of Iraqi generals would overthrow Hussein, but Western analysts and advisers did not support the idea of a general revolution that would throw the country and perhaps the region into wider chaos.

In the last hours of the war, as Coalition forces tracked down and destroyed Republican Guard armor and captured many Republican Guard troops, Hussein appeared to recognize that the only way he

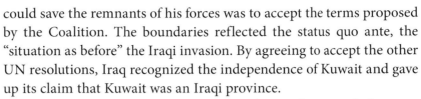

could save the remnants of his forces was to accept the terms proposed by the Coalition. The boundaries reflected the status quo ante, the "situation as before" the Iraqi invasion. By agreeing to accept the other UN resolutions, Iraq recognized the independence of Kuwait and gave up its claim that Kuwait was an Iraqi province.

The disparity in casualties between the Coalition and the Iraqi forces was striking. In the immediate aftermath of the war, the press began to report that the Iraqis had suffered 100,000 casualties. That number appeared to be based on the fact that original estimates had put the Iraqi forces opposing the Coalition at more than 500,000, and 86,000 had been taken prisoner. However, a year later, official Western sources came up with a more careful count. Putting together reliable estimates based on circumstantial evidence, analysts concluded that in total, less than 35,000 Iraqi military personnel were killed during Desert Shield and Desert Storm. About 19,000 were killed during 26 days of the air war, with another 4,000 killed by air attack in front line units. Another 10,000 or so appeared to have been killed during the land war. Despite the horrible pictures of the so-called highway of death, it was later learned that almost all of the troops trying to escape Kuwait by vehicle had fled on foot, abandoning their vehicles to be destroyed from the air and by tank fire.

By contrast, Coalition forces suffered lightly. U.S. forces suffered 148 killed in action, including 28 killed in one Scud hit on a barracks and 35 deaths from friendly fire. Other Coalition troops suffered 84 to 92 killed in action, with 318 wounded. Noncombat deaths, such as accidents and heart attacks, were almost as high, with 138 deaths from such causes among U.S. troops. In fact, the number injured in noncombat accidents far exceeded the number injured in combat. U.S. authorities reported some 3,000 noncombat injuries, but only 470 wounded in action. Some journalists claimed that had the troops stayed home, statistics showed that more of them would have died from natural causes and accidents in the United States than the total that died in their deployment to the gulf.

Analysts attributed the Coalition success to several decisive advantages: excellent training and practice, superior morale, better firepower, excellent logistics, and better weapons systems. The press and many in the public remembered the effect of the air war and the new types of guided missiles, and that perception held some truth. Schwarzkopf argued, and later military analysts agreed, that the traditional

KURDS AND KURDISTAN

The Kurdish people, like other ethnic groups living under the Ottoman Empire, expected to be granted an independent government following World War I. However, Britain insisted that the oil-rich Mosul district, which housed many Kurds, would remain in Iraq. Meanwhile, many Kurds also lived in Turkey, Syria, and Iran.

In 1974, the Iraqi government granted partial autonomy to the Kurdish region of northwestern Iraq, but many Kurds took up arms against Iraqi domination. The shah of Iran supported the rebels. Saddam Hussein repressed the 1975 uprising with bloody effectiveness, resulting in an estimated 60,000 military and civilian casualties. During the Iraq-Iran war in the 1980s, various Kurdish factions fought against domination from Baghdad. The so-called autonomy was brought to a brutal end.

Following the Persian Gulf War, in mid-March 1991, 100,000 Kurds organized in the Fursan, or Iraqi militia, changed sides and rose against Hussein. They hoped that, under American protection and with a supply of arms, they could fight for their age-old dream of a Kurdish state. However, Coalition members Turkey and Syria warned against weakening Iraqi control over the Kurdish regions. Turkey held an estimated 8 million Kurds, Syria had a half-million, and another 5 million lived in Iran. These countries feared that a strong Kurdish state in Iraq would spread instability across boundaries. Two weeks after the uprising began, by March 30, 1991, Iraqi forces crushed the rebellion. Kurds from whole villages and regions moved toward the Turkish border. An estimated 1.5 million, half the population of the region, became refugees.

issues of strategy, training, morale, firepower, and logistics had been extremely important. It was a mistake to think that air power alone had won the war.

American, French, and British soldiers all testified to the importance of intensive practice and training over several months prior to the beginning of the ground war. On the ground, troops built emplacements and barriers identical to those the Iraqis had and then repeatedly held drills on how to break through. By the time of the attack, they understood the problems and had solved them. Over and over, in interviews and in their memoirs, troops reported that when they

One factor working against Kurdish independence or greater autonomy was the fact that the Kurds could not coordinate their uprising with
Shiite Muslims in the South. More fundamentally, the United States
did not want to offend Turkey, nor did they want to so weaken the Iraqi
regime that Iran could overrun the country. It seemed that only Kurds
wanted an independent Kurdistan.

Kurdish women and children in the northern section of Iraq had long
been endangered by Saddam Hussein's regime, but following Operation
Desert Storm they were protected by a United Nations–sponsored resolution that forbade Iraqi planes from flying over the region. *(Defense
Imagery)*

finally attacked, it was very much like another practice drill, except for
the enemy casualty figures and surrendering troops.

The long bombardment from the air on Iraqi positions weakened
the enemy morale. At the same time, Coalition troops received support
from home—mail as well as access to telephones and even entertainment. When the surrenders of Iraqis began, Coalition troops realized
that most of the Iraqis did not believe in their cause and were glad to
see the end of the fighting.

The Iraqis had superior numbers of tanks, artillery, and armored
vehicles present on the ground in August. Even after the air war, they

Wounded U.S. servicepeople were evacuated by air to Germany for hospital care, helping to keep U.S. casualty figures low. *(DOD Defense Information Center, March ARB, California)*

had many that survived the bombing. Even so, Coalition firepower was superior, and not just in numbers. Reports from armored clashes showed that over and over, Coalition vehicles, with their night-fighting capability, longer-range weapons, and ammunition with higher penetrating power, simply outgunned Iraqi armor. Those differences helped account for the great disparity in frontline casualties between the Coalition and the Iraqis.

Even though some Coalition equipment was several years old, it tended to be superior to Iraqi equipment. Coalition communication, aerial surveillance, and electronic warfare aircraft effectively destroyed Iraqi radar equipment. Superior armor on Coalition tanks worked well. One innovation was reactive armor, that is, armor plated with explosives that deflect incoming enemy shells and their charges. Other special materials were effective against all kinds of enemy munitions. According to official sources, not a single M1 tank, the main U.S. battle tank, suffered penetration by enemy projectiles, although some suffered damage from friendly fire.

Coalition supply lines provided excellent support. Logistics for the Iraqis, on the other hand, suffered. The air attacks on bridges, railroads, and road traffic created such shortages that many Iraqi troops who surrendered reported that they had run low on food and even water, as well as ammunition and spare parts for equipment.

On top of all these technical aspects, analysts agreed that the war came out well for the Coalition because of excellent leadership and excellent performance of pilots, ship crews, and troops on the ground. Schwarzkopf had a clear vision of what he intended, and he communicated it quite well down through his command structure, as well as up through Colin Powell to the Joint Chiefs and through them to the president and his cabinet. Some analysts criticized Schwarzkopf's bursts of temper, but on the whole, communication worked well. Colin Powell helped assure that the political leaders provided necessary support to the military in the field, without trying to micromanage decisions in the field. From the military point of view,

In addition to high-tech missiles and air attack, artillery pieces like this M198 155 mm howitzer gave essential fire support to Coalition troops at the opening of the ground phase of the war. (*DOD Defense Information Center, March ARB, California*)

Only loosely and arbitrarily linked to the Persian Gulf War, *Three Kings,* starring George Clooney, was described as a "dark comedy" and hardly inspired much respect for a war that most Americans felt was a just cause. *(United Artists/Photofest)*

that represented a great improvement over the way the Vietnam War had been fought.

Alberto Bin, in *Desert Storm, A Forgotten War,* collected interview statements from soldiers who had been on the ground and from pilots. Sgt. Gino Pulizzi, who fought with the British Staffordshire Regiment, thought it was simply a matter of Coalition troops being better soldiers than the Iraqis. "We knew that we were better, man for man, than they would ever be," he said.

A U.S. Marine artillery officer, Lt. Col. Rob Rivers, identified the issue of skill. He thought the Iraqi equipment was good, but "It was badly maintained, and they didn't know how to use it properly . . . If we had the same equipment that the Iraqis had, we would have been able to use it more effectively." U.S. Army lieutenant Curtis Palmer agreed. "Trenches were poorly dug, usually not deep enough. They were deficient at basic military skills that go back to Caesar." An American pilot, Lt. Col. William Bryan, remarked, "They had the equipment, but they didn't have the resolve." The outcome had depended on people as much as it depended on weapons. And the will of the U.S. and Coalition troops had been superior.

But it was not enough to have won. Over the next months and years, the Coalition forces had to make sure that Iraq did not rebuild its forces to represent a threat to the region again. And the United Nations wanted to ensure that Iraq could not build or use weapons of mass destruction, particularly nuclear and chemical weapons. These jobs would be part of the long-term aftermath of the Persian Gulf War.

LONG-TERM
AFTERMATH

Although the ground phase of the Persian Gulf War ended quickly and decisively in favor of the Coalition, the long-term legacy of the war left a series of unresolved problems faced by world leadership and by the U.S. government during the following decade. One of the first problems arose from the terms of the cease-fire under which the United Nations insisted that Iraq not fly any fixed-wing aircraft north of 36° or south of 32° latitude lines. The terms of the cease-fire, however, did allow helicopter flights in these areas, a decision later criticized as allowing too much power to Hussein.

These restrictions appeared at first to provide the local dissidents, the Kurds in the North and the Shiite Muslims on the southern border with Iran, an opportunity to develop resistance to Baghdad. U.S. and British fighter aircraft would enforce these so-called no-fly zones. Even without any access to air power in those regions, however, Hussein was able to suppress both the rebellions within a month after the end of the Persian Gulf War. Later, British, American, and a small contingent of French and Dutch troops helped maintain a "safe haven" for returning Kurdish refugees in the northern no-fly zone, but when Kurdish leaders sought outside help in establishing independence, no countries in the former Coalition appeared willing to help.

Immediately following the conclusion of the war, units of the Republican Guard had conducted a brutal suppression of the Shiite rebellion. Thousands of Muslim clerics were arrested, and hundreds executed without trial. The guard units tied civilians to the front of their tanks as human shields, and civilians, including women and children, were shot. The city of Karbala was nearly destroyed. By March 26, 1991, however, the United States made it clear it would not intervene militarily to help the rebels in the south.

In the decade that followed the formal end of the Persian Gulf War, U.S. and British aircraft continued to patrol and enforce the no-fly zones. Frequently, Iraqi ground forces would turn on radar equipment and lock on the aircraft, in apparent preparation for launching surface-to-air missiles. In dozens of separate incidents, the aircraft bombed and destroyed the ground installations when such threatening radar contact was detected.

Among the conditions accepted by the Iraqis to obtain a cease-fire was a commitment to accept all 12 UN resolutions that had been passed as a result of the Iraqi invasion of Kuwait. One of those resolutions demanded that Iraq eliminate its nuclear, biological, and chemical weapons programs. Until those programs were eliminated, the

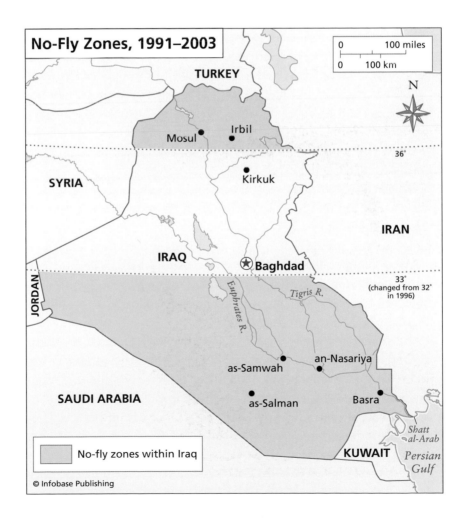

© Infobase Publishing

UN sanctions on oil export from and trade with Iraq would remain in place.

On April 4, 1991, the United Nations passed Resolution 687, requiring the certified destruction of all of Iraq's weapons of mass destruction. In order to prove that Iraq's programs had been eliminated, the United Nations Special Commission (UNSCOM) was set up to oversee an international team of investigators who would inspect sites in Iraq. Only when these UNSCOM inspectors were satisfied that all the weapons of mass destruction programs had been terminated would the United Nations raise the sanctions. Although this seemed like a clear and workable plan, it generated many difficulties.

As UNSCOM inspection teams arrived in Iraq, they soon found more than they had anticipated. It became clear from examining records and facilities that Iraq had had a very advanced nuclear weapons program prior to Desert Storm. Although many of the facilities had been destroyed, records showed that teams of Iraqi scientists and technicians had acquired and built many of the parts of nuclear weapons and had records of acquiring strategic nuclear material, including highly enriched uranium, to make the bombs. Over and over, Iraqi soldiers and officials put obstacles in the way of the UNSCOM inspectors, and a process that should have taken a few months stretched into years.

When UNSCOM declared that it would conduct surprise inspections of facilities that it chose, rather than those picked out by Iraq, Hussein established a special Concealment Operations Committee. The job of this group was to delay the teams, conceal evidence, and otherwise hamper the UNSCOM effort. And when UNSCOM had to give notice for inspections of certain warehouses and buildings, inspectors believed that Iraq would move truckloads of prohibited materials at night to prevent detection.

The inspectors found evidence of other secret activities of the Iraqi regime, including a school for the training of terrorists, covert procurement of components of ballistic missile systems and their launchers, and concealed chemical-weapons production facilities. The teams uncovered records of purchases of weapons from France. They found that the secret nuclear project called PC-3 had come very close to building a nuclear weapon on the eve of the Gulf War. They eventually uncovered records that detailed how the Iraqi government had planned a large-scale deception of the UNSCOM teams themselves by giving up certain equipment and information and hiding other materials and documents.

Even as the inspections went on, Iraq continued to act suspiciously, seemingly rebuilding its capabilities in chemical and biological warfare. Scott Ritter, an American who worked as an UNSCOM inspector until 1998 when he resigned in frustration, published an account claiming many violations. Ritter said that in 1994–1995, Iraq imported

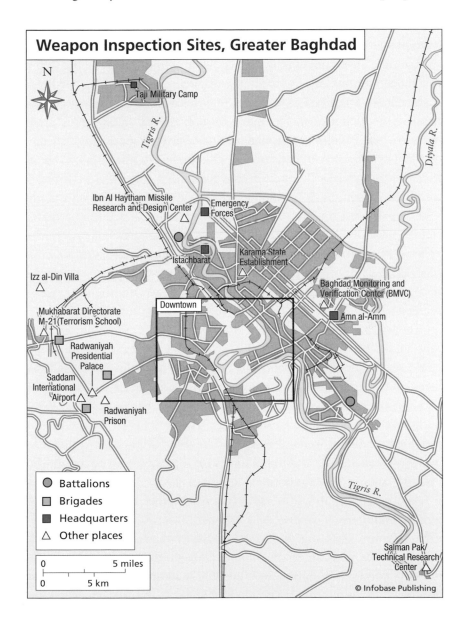

a chemical warfare plant under the disguise of building a pesticide facility. He showed that the Iraqi Special Security Organization worked to actively resist UNSCOM efforts to examine its facilities and records.

The long struggle between UNSCOM and Iraq over these weapons was not the only problem left over from the war. Over the years 1991–97, U.S. veterans of the Persian Gulf War reported a variety of physical and neurological symptoms, including weight loss, nausea, disorientation, and reduction in their immune systems. As medical researchers tried to identify the cause and nature of the problem, the press soon dubbed the collection of illnesses the "Gulf War syndrome." In this case, unlike "Vietnam syndrome," the term *syndrome* really did apply to a medical group of symptoms, the original meaning of the term.

Scientists produced a variety of theories as to the cause of the illnesses. One such was the fact that Coalition aircraft had targeted Iraqi chemical and biological weapons facilities. Perhaps some of the chemicals had escaped or had been mixed with the heavy smoke from the oil field fires to induce sickness. Another possibility was that the ammunition used in American tanks and artillery often included shells made with "depleted uranium." Although somewhat radioactive, the material is useless for nuclear weapons. Because it is extremely heavy for its volume, even heavier than lead, it makes an excellent armor-piercing shot. Perhaps, some argued, with all that radioactive material, troops had picked up radiation sickness. However, not all the symptoms seemed to coincide with those expected from radiation exposure.

Yet another theory suggested that the large group of vaccinations that soldiers underwent, including vaccination against anthrax, had combined to create the syndrome. Some journalists even blamed the fact that American troops consumed vast quantities of diet soda that had not been refrigerated. The U.S. Veterans Administration dealt with thousands of medical claims from troops through the 1990s and provided treatment where it was called for. By the end of the 20th century, researchers still continued to debate the cause and nature of the mysterious Gulf War syndrome.

Another post–Gulf War issue was whether or not the American public would react as they had following the Vietnam War, shunning veterans, rejecting military commitments overseas, and thereby placing limits on U.S. foreign policy. Policy analysts and journalists debated whether the "Vietnam syndrome" had been eliminated by the Gulf War.

A U.S. Army cargo truck is getting a special coat of chemical-resistant paint prior to being sent to the Persian Gulf. The truck is a decontamination vehicle that was to be used should the Iraqis release toxic chemicals. *(Defense Imagery)*

By far the most serious long-term consequence of the Persian Gulf War had less to do with American reactions than with the reactions of many in the Muslim world. In 1990, the Saudi Arabians and the Arabs of the smaller gulf states had feared that Hussein would extend his conquest from Kuwait into their territories. His armed forces would have overwhelmed their defenses if he attempted it in August of 1990. King Fahd of Saudi Arabia had at first been reluctant to accept non-Islamic, Western forces into his country in any number. After assurances from General Schwarzkopf and other U.S. leaders that the troops would scrupulously respect local culture, religion, customs, and laws, Fahd allowed the buildup. On the whole, the Americans kept their promise, restricting the troops in their recreation and in their fraternization with the local population to conform to the standards of Islamic society.

When the war concluded, American and other troops left Saudi Arabia, but the United States continued to maintain a presence in the country, protecting air bases and keeping ready in case Hussein should once again launch an unprovoked attack. Saudi Arabia is the location of the two most holy cities in the Muslim world, Mecca and Medina.

VIETNAM SYNDROME

One issue that haunted the Persian Gulf War was the so-called Vietnam syndrome. Journalists had developed the phrase to refer to the fact that following the Vietnam War, in the late 1970s and through the 1980s, the American public adopted an isolationist attitude similar to that following World War I. Disillusioned in the objectives and implementation of the Vietnam War, and believing that U.S. troops had gone to Vietnam because of incorrect, immoral, or unwise decisions of the political leadership, the American public and the media tended to reject the idea of committing troops overseas.

Saddam Hussein apparently counted on American public pressure to prevent a commitment of troops to defend either Kuwait or Saudi Arabia. Even after polls in the United States showed support for military action in the Persian Gulf, policy makers feared that if casualty figures climbed, that support would diminish and there would be pressure to end the involvement quickly.

Another aspect of the Vietnam syndrome had been a rejection by the media and the public of military personnel themselves. Some Americans had shunned veterans of the Vietnam War, rather than welcoming them home as heroes. But during the Persian Gulf War, the American public generally showed intense support for the troops overseas, through demonstrations, ceremonies, and flag and yellow-ribbon displays.

It appeared that some aspects of Vietnam syndrome no longer dominated American public attitudes. The fact that U.S. casualties in the Persian Gulf War were extremely light appeared to contribute to the

The prophet Muhammad had lived in Arabia, and the Arabian Peninsula was the birthplace of Islam. For religious Muslims of all sects, Arabia itself was sacred ground.

Militant Islamic fundamentalists who sought to build a following seized on the U.S. presence in Saudi Arabia as a grievance. Most notably, Osama bin Laden emerged as a leader using this issue, rallying a following called "Islamists" or "international jihadists" by outside analysts. *Jihad* is an Arabic word that means "struggle," but it has come to be applied in common usage to the notion of a "holy war" conducted by Muslims. A member of a wealthy Saudi Arabian family, bin Laden had used part of his fortune to establish agencies

sustained support for the war in 1991. Even so, policy makers remained very cautious about committing large numbers of U.S. troops to action overseas in peacekeeping roles. They remained unsure whether the Vietnam syndrome had entirely vanished.

President Bush receives a salute from Gen. Norman Schwarzkopf and his troops during the Desert Storm Homecoming Parade in Washington, D.C., on July 8, 1991. Unlike returning Vietnam War veterans, U.S. troops were welcomed home with many celebrations following Operation Desert Storm. *(Defense Imagery)*

in Afghanistan to provide military and humanitarian aid to the guerrilla fighters there who sought to evict Soviet forces in the 1980s. He had received help from both Pakistan and the U.S. Central Intelligence Agency in building up a strong Islamic resistance to the Soviet presence.

Using his private fortune and funds from supporters, Osama bin Laden built a large organization, attracting volunteers from many Arab and Muslim countries. The international force that he built up remained supportive of his ideas through the 1990s, and he converted it into a terrorist organization, known as al-Qaeda ("the base"), dedicated to the eradication of non-Islamic influence, or "infidel presence,"

Terrorist attacks remained a threat to U.S. forces stationed in the Middle East as shown by the truck bombing of Khobar Towers in Saudi Arabia in June 1996, when 19 U.S. service personnel were killed. *(Defense Imagery)*

in the holy lands. He funded training camps in Afghanistan, Sudan, and other countries.

Terrorism continued to be a threat to Americans in the CENT-COM region during the 1990s. Five Americans died on November 15, 1995, when a car bomb detonated in front of a Saudi national guard office in the Saudi capital city of Riyadh. When on June 25, 1996, a terrorist driving a tank truck filled with explosives detonated near a U.S. residential complex, Khobar Towers, in Dhahran, Saudi Arabia, the continuing price paid by Americans for engagement in that part of the world came home again. A total of 19 U.S. service members were killed in that attack. Some 5,000 U.S. troops and support personnel were transferred from Dhahran to a more secure base in Saudi Arabia, at al Kharj. Then on August 7, 1998, terrorists later linked to Osama bin Laden's organization set off bombs at the U.S. embassies in Nairobi, Kenya, and in Dar Es Salaam, Tanzania. President Clinton responded to this attack a few days later with missile attacks on an abandoned and vacated training camp in Afghanistan and a pharma-

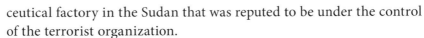

ceutical factory in the Sudan that was reputed to be under the control of the terrorist organization.

Repercussions from the role of the United States in the Middle East continued. Investigators traced an attack on the U.S. destroyer *Cole* on October 12, 2000, in the harbor of Aden in Yemen to the same organization of radical Islamists headed by Osama bin Laden. On February 26, 1993, a truck bomb exploded in the basement of New York City's World Trade Center and killed six people. At that time not much attention was paid to a possible link to bin Laden. But when on September 11, 2001, there were disastrous attacks by hijacked aircraft on the World Trade Center and the Pentagon—catastrophes that took approximately 3,000 lives—American investigators soon traced the plot and the perpetrators to bin Laden's group, al-Qaeda. As a consequence, the United States launched an international effort called Enduring Freedom to track down and destroy the terrorist organization in Afghanistan in 2001–02.

This series of terrorist incidents makes it quite clear that one of the consequences of the Persian Gulf War was to provide a focus for anti-American feelings among fundamentalist Muslims who found bin Laden's position and tactics attractive. The police action of the United States in the Persian Gulf began with the intention to protect the world's oil supply from a ruthless takeover attempt and to preserve the independence of Kuwait. In the long run, the Persian Gulf War had unforeseen consequences that would shape vital issues of security for the United States and the rest of the world. But the issue remained: How would America view sending its youth off to police the world in the 21st century?

Following the terrorist attack of September 11, 2001, the question seemed answered with a renewed surge of patriotic support for a vigorous pursuit of the perpetrators and a defeat of the Taliban regime in Afghanistan that harbored al-Qaeda. In 2002, U.S. president George W. Bush and British prime minister Tony Blair sought support for more forceful international action against Saddam Hussein. Intelligence information confirmed that Hussein had retained some stores of chemical weapons, but despite extensive searching, no evidence of continuing work on nuclear weapons after 1998 could be uncovered. President Bush called on the American people and the U.S. Congress for support in using U.S. troops to enforce the UN resolutions prohibiting Iraqi work on weapons of mass destruction. As Americans debated the topic, the challenge was to decide whether such a use of force conformed to American ideals and whether it was necessary to American self-interest and security. In 2002, the support was there, with a majority believing that Hussein's regime in Iraq continued to threaten both American principles and American security.

WEAPONS
AND TACTICS

In the Persian Gulf War, as in any war, tactics and broader strategy were shaped by the state of weapons technology. As the tools of war and the uses of available resources for defense have changed over time, the particular way a war is fought changes from the way it was fought in past wars. However, some of the basic principles of war have always remained the same. The specific weapons developed in a specific period affect how the principles of war are employed.

As commanders plan ahead and develop larger strategies, they have to keep in mind the sorts of weapons and defenses they can call on and that the enemy will use. In the Persian Gulf War, weapons technology shaped immediate battlefield tactics and the larger strategy of both sides. It also affected the outcome and the long and bitter arguments in the aftermath of the war.

Although there were many new weapons in the arsenals of both sides, including some that had never been used before in a war, the methods and ideas that both sides used reflected concepts of warfare that had been developed in earlier wars. Coalition forces sought to gather intelligence, to destroy the enemy's ability to communicate between commanders and the field, and to use the element of surprise. These tactics had been part of warfare since ancient times. Modern technology changed the ways these traditional methods and ideas were carried out, but the principles behind their use were as old as organized warfare.

Similarly, Saddam Hussein had several new weapons at his disposal. He did what he could to structure strong defenses around the Iraqi positions, interfere with the Coalition's ability to gather information, and come up with ways to divide the Coalition arrayed against him, by playing on their political divisions. Again, these ideas were not new, but the technology that the Iraqis used to try to achieve the goals was in some cases very new.

In the Persian Gulf War, the American and Coalition forces knew that they would be fighting against an extremely large and very well-equipped Iraqi army. The divisions of the Republican Guard had at their disposal vast numbers of modern Soviet tanks. Hundreds of thousands of foot soldiers, although less dedicated and disciplined, made up a massive army. That army had years of experience in the long war between Iraq and Iran.

Saddam Hussein's forces had used poison gas in the war against Iran, and Coalition commanders feared that they might do so again. So American and other Coalition troops traveled equipped not only with gas masks but heavy clothing that would keep poison or irritant gas from reaching skin surfaces.

Of course, in the desert, such clothing was a burden. Furthermore, when troops stopped at a hastily erected compound, they would have to take shelter in gas-resistant tents. Later, when it was learned that the Iraqis had chosen not to deploy any poison gas, troops still wondered why they had developed a strange variety of illness symptoms. After the war, the press began to call the symptoms the "Persian Gulf Syndrome," meaning a disease that had not been diagnosed. Various theories suggested that the symptoms had developed from inhaled smoke in the battlefield, from microscopic organisms found in Iraq, or from wearing the oppressively hot anti–poison gas equipment.

Coalition forces understood that if they could gain air superiority before the ground offensive took place, they would have a better chance of driving the Iraqi army out of Kuwait quickly and with minimum casualties to their own side. Furthermore, with command of the air, the Coalition forces would be in a better position to gather intelligence and to interrupt and destroy the Iraqi ability to communicate between headquarters and the forces in the field.

That is why, during the bombing phase of Operation Desert Storm that began on January 16, 1991, American, French, and other Coalition aircraft targeted the Iraqi airforce and its ground facilities. The Iraqi response was to fly more than 100 of its own aircraft out of the country, while just about an equal number were destroyed or damaged on the ground or in the air. Within days, the Coalition had control of the air. Part of the effort went beyond attacking Iraqi aircraft and included thorough destruction of the Iraqi radar installations and the

COMMAND OF THE AIR

Airplanes had played an important role in warfare soon after they were developed. In World War I (1914–18), small fighter planes were used as observation posts to spot enemy positions, then to shoot down observation balloons, and later to drive off enemy airplanes. By the end of the war, some planes had become dedicated to the purpose of bombing and strafing (that is, shooting from the air) against enemy ground positions.

In Italy during World War I, General Giulio Douhet was in command of an aviation battalion. He studied the use of aircraft and soon after the war completed an influential study entitled *Command of the Air*. This book was translated into many languages and studied widely by military around the world in the 1920s and 1930s. It influenced military thinking for decades. Douhet spelled out how it was important for military forces, early in any war, to gain "command of the air." By that he meant that air forces should be used first, to destroy enemy air forces, airfields, airplane production facilities, and antiaircraft ground weapons. When this had been accomplished, an attacking army would be able to use the third dimension of the airspace above an enemy so that any point within the enemy's territory could be attacked, not just the ground front.

This simple concept shaped the development and use of air forces in World War II and in succeeding wars and played an extremely important role in the Persian Gulf War. The whole bombing phase of Operation Desert Storm was devoted to implementing Douhet's concept.

associated antiaircraft weapons that would protect Iraqi forces from Coalition air attack.

Once the Coalition forces had gained control of the air, they focused on attacking the Iraqi command, control, and intelligence facilities. This meant that headquarters buildings of the Iraqi army, government buildings housing intelligence services, and all communications facilities, such as radio and telephone systems, were destroyed with carefully targeted bombs. These attacks were made using the newly developed "smart bombs" that were guided to their targets, sometimes even through particular windows in buildings, by using small television transmitters in the weapons themselves.

The Coalition air forces also used traditional "gravity" bombs or "dumb bombs" that were simply dropped over large targets in hopes that they would hit the specific facilities. Attacking command, control, and communications systems had always been part of warfare, but now it was being carried out with late 20th-century technology. One unique part of the air attack was the first employment in warfare of the Tomahawk cruise missile, fired from U.S. warships stationed in the Persian Gulf.

But it was not only the high technology of the bombs that mattered. Rather, it was the sheer scale of the bombing. On the first night of the air war, it was estimated that Coalition forces dropped more than 18,000 tons of high explosives.

The air attack before the ground invasion was effective. Estimates of destruction of Iraqi equipment included more than 1,300 tanks, about 1,100 heavy artillery pieces, and 850 armored personnel carriers. Even having sustained these heavy losses, however, the Iraqis still had a formidable armored force left, with about 3,000 tanks, 2,000 pieces of artillery, and 2,000 personnel carriers. This was no ragtag guerrilla army but a modern, well-equipped, experienced and well-trained army that had plenty of time to dig in and prepare.

The awesome power of so-called smart bombs can be seen here in the damage done to one of the Iraqi bunkers hit by Allied forces during Operation Desert Storm. *(Defense Imagery)*

THE U.S. NAVY IN THE PERSIAN GULF WAR

Ships of the U.S. Navy participated in three basic ways in Operation Desert Shield and Operation Desert Storm. One way was to support the "feint," or false attack, of an amphibious assault, by sending helicopters and other naval aircraft, together with some landing craft, in maneuvers off the coast of Kuwait.

A second way was the launching of more than 100 Tomahawk missiles. Originally developed as a long-range sea-launched cruise missile with nuclear weapons for possible use in a major war with the Soviet Union, the Tomahawk carried conventional high explosives. Known as the Tomahawk Land Assault Missile, these weapons could reach targets hundreds of miles inland, including targets in Baghdad. Although only reasonably accurate, and although the Iraqi defenders were able to shoot down some of them, they still proved their effectiveness.

The third major way that the Navy supported the operations ashore was through the use of carrier-based aircraft. With very limited access to airfields in the region, naval aircraft were the backbone of the air assault. As part of the effort to destroy the Iraqi ground-based antiaircraft and radar installations, U.S. Navy drones or unmanned aircraft were launched, drawing radar and fire from the Iraqis. Then the ground facilities would be destroyed. A special HARM air-to-ground missile that would target radar installations proved very useful against the Iraqi radar equipment. The navy's carrier-based EA-6B Prowler aircraft, devoted to electronic countermeasures, also proved valuable. It helped protect Coalition aircraft by sending jamming signals against the Iraqi radar.

In addition to the previously mentioned carrier-based planes, U.S. Marine AV-8 Harriers and F/A-18 Hornets used Maverick missiles, while the navy A-6 Intruders used their FLIR (infrared-heat seeking) and 500-pound laser-guided bombs in strikes against Iraqi tanks and armored personnel carriers.

As Saddam Hussein and his commanders considered their options, they had several weapons and defensive tactics that technology had made possible. One was the use of the modified Soviet ground-to-ground (or surface-to-surface) SS-1 missiles, known as Scuds. Whether or not they had been modified to achieve the long range of 590 miles, it was clear that they could be used to attack Coalition troops assembling in Saudi Arabia. The Scud missiles were mounted on heavy, multi-axle transporter-erector-launcher vehicles so that they could be moved to remote locations in the desert, fired, and then moved to a new spot before the Coalition forces could locate and destroy the transport equipment.

Hussein had developed quite an arsenal of other modern weapons. These included the experimental supergun designed by Gerald Bull, the Canadian engineer. If it had been completed, the supergun could possibly have had a range of several hundred miles. The assembled gun was only discovered after Iraq was defeated and weapons inspectors toured the country, looking for evidence of nuclear, biological, and chemical weapons. Hussein also had extensive manufacturing capabilities for poison gas and had a secret program for the development of nuclear weapons. The exact extent of the nuclear program itself became very controversial in the mid- and late 1990s. Evidence uncovered much later suggests that the nuclear weapon project was discontinued in the

MIM-104 Patriot tactical air defense systems are positioned for protection of a nearby air base in the aftermath of Operation Desert Storm. (*Defense Imagery*)

late 1990s, but no one outside Iraq knew the extent of the weapons of mass destruction arsenal when the Persian Gulf War began.

In a surprise move, Hussein tried to use Scud missiles to politically divide the forces arrayed against Iraq. Hussein hoped that by attacking Israel, the Israeli air force would retaliate against Iraq. Early in the air campaign against Iraq, the Iraqis fired several Scuds that exploded in the Israeli cities of Tel Aviv and Haifa. If the Israelis had retaliated, the Coalition would probably have broken up, because numerous Muslim countries in the Coalition would refuse to fight on the same side with Israel. In this way, the choice of weapons shaped not only tactical thinking but also the larger Iraqi strategy at the level of international politics. However, this strategy failed because the United States prevailed upon Israel not to retaliate. In exchange for this agreement, the United States provided Israel with some Patriot missile batteries.

Patriot missiles, which had been developed in the United States as antiaircraft defensive missiles, were first employed in the Persian Gulf War as a defense against the Iraqi Scud missiles. The Patriot missile batteries helped encourage the Israelis that at least they had some defense against incoming Scuds. Patriot batteries based in Saudi Arabia were also used, with mixed success, in shooting down Iraqi Scud missiles that had been aimed at American military bases where troops were assembling for the ground attack on Iraq. In fact, after the war, a lasting controversy continued to rage about whether or not the Patriot missiles had been very effective against the Scuds. Even a partially destroyed Scud, or parts from an exploded Patriot falling from the sky, could be very dangerous to troops or civilians on the ground near the target area. As a consequence of the Patriot versus Scud experience, American technologists and weapons developers later worked to improve the quality of antimissile missiles.

During the air campaign against Iraq, some small Special Forces units of the United States air-dropped into Iraq in order to help identify the temporary locations of some of the Scud launchers, so that those missile launching sites could be targeted by Coalition fighter-bombers. This infiltration tactic was quite secret at the time, and later reports indicated that it had some limited success in helping to track down and destroy Scud launchers. The harrowing stories of some of these Special Forces units, and the methods they employed in hiding from Iraqi patrols, made for exciting narratives when they were later published.

An A-10A Thunderbolt II attack aircraft, familiarly known as the "Warthog," proved valuable in Operation Desert Storm by providing support for ground troops and by knocking out tanks with its powerful Gatling gun. *(Defense Imagery)*

Gathering the intelligence about Iraq was made more difficult by a defensive tactic that the Iraqis used. They set fire to hundreds of oil wells and tank farms in Kuwait. These fires caused vast clouds of black smoke, which to an extent concealed the movement of troops and equipment on the ground in Kuwait and in Iraq in the region near Kuwait. Although smoke from fires had often obscured ground targets from aircraft in previous wars, the intentional igniting of oil well fires as a defensive weapon was another "first" in the Persian Gulf War.

Despite the vast clouds of smoke, the Coalition forces had some knowledge of the sort of defenses the Iraqis had prepared. Along the long border with Saudi Arabia and the shorter border between Kuwait and Saudi Arabia, they had prepared miles of "sand berms"—long mounds of sand that had been bulldozed to prevent a rapid movement of armored vehicles such as tanks and armored personnel carriers.

Another defense that the Iraqis employed was to use some of their tanks as simple stationary artillery. Drawing on their large supply of Soviet-built tanks, they drove many of them to the defensive perimeter in southern Iraq and then partially buried them in pits. The tanks' exposed parts were covered with sand so that they would not be easily identified from the air, but leaving the turret and gun exposed; the

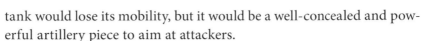

tank would lose its mobility, but it would be a well-concealed and pow-erful artillery piece to aim at attackers.

However, when Iraqi tanks pulled out from their dug-in positions, they would lose their concealment. Then they could be attacked from the air by the "tank-busting" Warthog aircraft, the A-10 Thunderbolt. Sometimes the panicked Iraqi troops would abandon the half-buried tank and flee on foot.

Knowing that the Iraq army was large, with an estimated 400,000 troops stationed in and around Kuwait, that it had thousands of tanks, that the Republican Guard units were well-disciplined and well-equipped, General Schwarzkopf developed in secret the "Hail Mary" strategy that was later so much admired, once it was revealed. The plan consisted of several elements. One element was using a marine force, equipped with amphibious vehicles, to make a "feint," or false attack, toward Kuwait City itself. Backed by U.S. Navy ships that fired missiles as if preparing for an amphibious landing, the attack seemed very real. The feint drew Iraqi attention and forces to focus on defending Kuwait City against forces from the sea. At the same time, a large armored force was moved along the Iraqi border on the Saudi side, to the west and north, in complete secrecy far beyond the main defended sector of the Iraqi border.

This wide swing out to the left, or west, was like the "Hail Mary" play in football, in which a wide receiver swings far out to receive a pass, and the quarterback supposedly offers a silent prayer that, despite the distance, the receiver will catch the ball. General Schwarz-kopf, a former football player, appeared to revel in the use of the term, and once it was fully under way, press officers explained the maneuver in briefings held at bases back in Arabia for news report-ers. The plan looked good on paper, and it turned out to look good on the ground.

After the quick move through the desert, the forces breached the lightly defended sand berms inside the western Iraqi border, using armored bulldozers and then rushed through with tanks and person-nel carriers of the two U.S. paratroop divisions, the 82nd and 101st Airborne Divisions, and armored infantry troops of the VII Corps and XVIII Corps. As the surviving Iraqi infantry defenders fled from the advancing armored columns, they soon began to surrender by the thousands. It was clear that the Hail Mary surprise attack had some spectacular initial success.

This basic tactic helped account for the rapid defeat of the Iraqi army. Even though the plan was well thought out and well carried out, of course it was not without casualties. Despite the destruction of much of the Iraqi command and control facilities, the Iraqi Republican Guard was able to field some armored units and engage in a furious night battle on February 26 with the 24th Infantry Division from VII Corps. This was only one of several quick and bloody engagements of armored forces to the west of Kuwait in the Iraqi approaches to Baghdad.

The use of new weapons and the adaptive use of civilian facilities for defense made the short four-day war both spectacular and

WMD

The American public first became familiar with the term *WMD* during the Persian Gulf War. These letters stood for "weapons of mass destruction." Defense planners and specialists had used the term as shorthand to describe three types of weapons that were capable of killing masses of people. These included chemical and biological weapons such as poison gas and methods of dispersing germs that spread diseases. The term also covered nuclear weapons, both those that detonated like the atomic bombs used at Hiroshima and Nagasaki at the end of World War II and so-called dirty bombs that would spread radioactive material that would be fatal over a wide area.

Sometimes the phrase *WMD* was used without much in the way of explanation or definition, and some in the public may have come to think that the term referred only to nuclear weapons. After the Persian Gulf War, weapons inspectors under UN orders sought to track down and identify all WMD sites inside Iraq. Stockpiles of older chemical weapons were found and destroyed, but it was difficult for the inspectors to learn whether the Iraqi regime continued its program to develop nuclear weapons.

The Iraqis made it impossible for the inspectors to visit all suspected sites in the country. Experts, journalists, and foreign governments could not tell whether the Iraqis concealed the sites because they had nuclear weapons under development or whether they simply wanted outsiders to be in doubt over the question so that neighboring countries would be intimidated by Iraqi power. In later years, inspectors found only evidence of chemical WMD, not nuclear WMD.

extremely controversial. Scuds had proven Patriots to be less effective than American weapons specialists had hoped. Collateral damage shocked Americans and other members of the Coalition. The defenses against poison gas, gas that was not employed in the war, may have contributed to the lasting sicknesses from which many Persian Gulf War veterans suffered. The pollution of the air from some 600 oilwell fires spread across the Indian Ocean. The damage to oil wells caused destruction that would cost billions of dollars to repair. Cleanup costs of the oil spilled into the gulf itself also ran into the billions of dollars.

Since the object of the war had been the liberation of Kuwait, and since the Coalition troops from many countries had joined the effort with that goal in mind, the war did not go beyond the liberation of Kuwait. General Schwarzkopf, on orders from Washington, accepted surrender of Iraqi troops without a final defeat of the Iraqi army. That in itself left a dangerous legacy, as UN members worried that Hussein would secretly rebuild his WMD capability, including poison gas, chemical weapons, and nuclear weapons. So the weapons themselves not only contributed to the tactics, strategy, and outcome of the war, but planted the seeds for future conflict.

PEACEKEEPING IN THE 1990S AND PERSIAN GULF WAR LEGACIES

Like most wars, the Persian Gulf War left a legacy of problems and lessons for the generations that followed. One issue was how Americans would react to further efforts at policing the world or participating in peacekeeping operations.

Although the term is often used without a precise definition, as far as the United Nations is concerned, *peacekeeping operations* are a special category of semimilitary actions. In peacekeeping operations, usually a small force of lightly armed soldiers from a number of countries acts as a military presence to maintain an existing peace between two or more conflicting military groups. In most cases, the UN peacekeepers do not enter a country without the consent of the parties in conflict, and their usual function is to keep the antagonists apart. Typically, the UN troops maintain border posts, conduct inspections of vehicles, do surveillance of military facilities and weapons, and sometimes serve as police patrols to prevent ethnic or religious groups from clashing.

Between 1948 and 1998, the UN Security Council established a total of 49 peacekeeping operations. Most of these (36) were established between 1988 and 1998. In the 50 years of peacekeeping following its founding, the United Nations called on soldiers from 111 countries, including some very small nations, to help in these operations. Often, the soldiers and police from various states wore blue helmets with a UN symbol while continuing to wear their national uniforms.

Brig. Gen. Frank Libutti, Commander Joint Task Force Operation Provide Relief, greets children in Somalia, a United Nations–sponsored operation to aid the strife-torn and starving peoples of Somalia. *(Defense Imagery)*

In some of the "blue helmet operations" the United States played no part, and in others, the number of U.S. troops was less than that provided by smaller countries, such as Fiji or Nepal. However, the United States participated on a large scale in two major UN blue helmet operations in the 1990s, one in Somalia, on the northeast "horn" of Africa, and the other in the troubled ethnic fighting on the Balkan peninsula of Europe. Both served to test the reaction of the American public to overseas commitments of U.S. forces.

The Somalia operation fell within the area of responsibility of CENTCOM, the same military command previously headed by General Schwarzkopf in the earlier Persian Gulf War. The national government in Somalia collapsed following the departure of the dictator Mohamed Siad Barre on January 26, 1991. The country divided and became organized under military warlords fighting a civil war with constantly shifting alignments. To relieve starvation, CENTCOM began to provide food in Operation Provide Relief in August 1992. As part of that operation, groups of U.S. troops went in to establish communications, conduct airfield surveys, and provide for flight clearances and to coordinate assistance with nongovernmental relief agencies. Provide Relief used some 858 personnel and delivered nearly 20,000 tons of food and supplies in late 1992.

CENTCOM also helped move a 500-man Pakistani force of blue-helmet peacekeepers to Mogadishu, the capital of Somalia, in September 1992. However, it soon became clear that the relief supplies were not getting to the starving people who needed them, so President George H. W. Bush ordered a new operation, Restore Hope, in support of UN Security Council Resolution 794. CENTCOM led a multinational coalition of troops in United Task Force, or UNITAF. The job of UNITAF was to provide security at transportation and food distribution centers and to keep the relief organizations and convoys secure from raids and looting. Meanwhile, Provide Relief continued, bringing in more food.

UNITAF divided southern Somalia into nine relief sectors, and under a UN organization established as UNISOM II in March 1993, the U.S. forces shared responsibility with forces from other nations. American troops made up 25,800 of the 38,300 personnel. The other 12,000 or so came from many countries, with Canada, France, Italy, Morocco, Australia, Belgium, and Botswana each in control of a region. Troops from Pakistan, Malaysia, Nigeria, and other nations assisted in the peacekeeping. The forces under UNISOM II not only provided security but worked on all sorts of community improvement, relief, and humanitarian efforts, such as drilling water wells, building hospitals and schools, and repairing and building roads. Medical personnel treated thousands of Somalis.

Although the UN troops established a flow of relief and some security in the countryside, the capital city of Mogadishu remained chaotic. One warlord, Gen. Mohamed Farah Aideed, led the hostility to the presence of UNISOM forces. On June 5, 1993, Aideed's forces ambushed and attacked Pakistani peacekeepers who were trying to confiscate weapons, leaving 24 of the Pakistanis dead. UNISOM troops rescued survivors. Trouble continued through the summer of 1993. A remotely detonated mine killed four U.S. military policemen on August 8. Later in August, President Bill Clinton's secretary of defense, Les Aspin, ordered deployment of U.S. Task Force Rangers to Somalia to help enforce UN resolutions there.

In September 1993, Somali forces attacked Nigerian peacekeepers. The U.S. Rangers succeeded in capturing a few of the Somali leaders. However, on September 25, three American crew members were killed after Somali militiamen shot down their helicopter, and Somalis killed other Rangers attempting a rescue. On October 3, Task Force Ranger captured six of Aideed's lieutenants, but as they withdrew, Somalis shot down two more helicopters. In the shootdown and the battle that followed, 300 Somalis and 18 Rangers were killed. UN forces, including Pakistanis and Malaysians, extracted surviving Ranger forces. This incident became the subject of a movie based on a best-selling book, *Black Hawk Down*. President Clinton ordered the deployment of more troops but at the same time announced that all U.S. forces would be withdrawn early in 1994. The American forces all pulled out by March 25, 1994. U.S. ships helped in the withdrawal of other peacekeepers from Somalia, including those from Italy, Pakistan, Bangladesh, Zimbabwe, and India.

American popular and press reaction to the events in Somali divided sharply. Some believed the United States had not been properly prepared for "mission creep," in which American forces took on a larger and larger military role, and that a much more powerful force had been required from the beginning. Others felt that the effort by the United Nations to establish peacekeeping forces in Somalia was a bad idea, as there was no peace to keep.

Officers from *(left to right)* the U.S. Marines, the United Arab Emirates, and Pakistan sit in the front row of a security briefing at the airport in Mogadishu, Somalia, part of Operation Restore Hope in which coalition forces tried to help establish civil order in Somalia in 1993. *(Defense Imagery)*

Traditionally, UN blue helmets went into areas where there was at least a promise that the two sides would accept the peacekeepers as independent and neutral in the local dispute, pledging not to take sides between the hostile camps. But in Somalia, the warlords, particularly Aideed, had never agreed to accept the peacekeepers. In this circumstance, some argued, what was required was not a lightly armed peacekeeping force, but either a hands-off approach or a full-scale invasion and occupation of the country with heavy weapons and a military defeat of the warlords. Because the United Nations had not endorsed such a course, the result was the tragic death of peacekeepers from many countries.

Americans' revulsion at the deaths of U.S. troops and the spectacle of Somali militiamen dragging dead U.S. soldiers through the streets of Mogadishu behind vehicles suggested to some observers that the Vietnam syndrome still held. Americans, it seemed, had accepted the number of 145 Americans killed in battle in the Persian Gulf War but could not tolerate similar numbers in small, inconclusive police actions like that in Somalia. Furthermore, the peacekeeping action in Somalia did not meet the long-standing justifications that Americans accepted for warfare: an important issue of self-interest or an important principle of American idealism. It simply seemed that U.S. troops, along with those of other nations, had been plunged ill prepared into a conflict in which Americans had no stake. The president was criticized for an apparently fuzzy grasp of the situation.

Through the 1990s, U.S. forces also participated in peacekeeping operations in Europe. Based on UN Resolution 1031, a special force was created to keep the peace in the republics of the former Yugoslavia that were being torn apart by vicious civil wars along ethnic and religious lines. The North Atlantic Treaty Organization (NATO) took the lead in implementing the General Framework for Peace, which had been negotiated in Dayton, Ohio, and signed in Paris in December 1995. Known as the Dayton Accords, this agreement provided what was missing in Somalia, a basic agreement for peace that could then be "kept" or enforced by troops and military police. The peacekeepers were to keep apart competing armed forces in Bosnia.

That republic was divided between ethnic Croats and ethnic Serbs, each of whom had their own armies and both of whom terrorized and tried to exterminate Bosnian Muslims. The peacekeeping group, known as the Implementation Force, or IFOR, started its one-year mis-

Troops from Holland, France, Germany, and the United States participate in the activation ceremony for the Stabilization Force (SFOR) in Bosnia-Herzegovina, assigned to enforce the conditions there as called for by the Dayton Peace Accords. *(Defense Imagery)*

sion on December 20, 1995, with more than 60,000 troops. IFOR set up patrols to watch a demilitarized boundary line between the two forces, inspected heavy weapon sites, repaired bridges, and opened the airport in the partially destroyed city of Sarajevo.

A year later, IFOR was replaced by SFOR, or Stabilization Force. SFOR included not only NATO troops but also non-NATO soldiers from many countries, including Russia, Finland, Bulgaria, and Sweden. The blue-helmet SFOR forces totaled about 32,000 troops, later reduced to about 20,000. One of SFOR's missions was to track down and arrest a number of war criminals some Serbian and Croat officers who had been accused of leading their troops in the committing of atrocities such as mass executions of civilians, organized rape, and killing of prisoners of war. On the whole, the SFOR forces made very few arrests of the accused war criminals, but maintained a troubled peace. With only an occasional casualty, most of which were the results of accidents, the U.S. presence in the SFOR force drew little attention from the American press.

The operations in the former Yugoslavia raised new questions about the legacy of the Persian Gulf War in American public opinion. It appeared that President Clinton hesitated to engage U.S. ground forces in military situations that could result in casualties. Although in 1999 Clinton committed U.S. airplanes and personnel to intensive bombing to force the Serbs to accept an agreement regarding the province of Kosovo, some American observers and others around the world questioned the wisdom of such an approach.

To many, it appeared that the United States had decided that it would no longer put its troops in harm's way to achieve foreign policy goals. The easy victory in Iraq in 1991 appeared to leave a mixed legacy. On the one hand, the United States was increasingly being called upon to help police the trouble spots in the world. The United States, with its modern weapons technology and well-trained military, seemed to be the policing nation that would be called upon to assist in new trouble

KOSOVO, 1999

Although the Dayton Peace Accords of 1995 appeared to quiet the civil war in Bosnia, those accords left unsettled a burning issue in the Kosovo province of Serbia. There, both Serbs and ethnic Albanians kept strict segregation from each other, and each group distrusted the other. Next door, Albania supported the movement inside Kosovo to make that province independent under the rule of the ethnic Albanians. The Albanians in Kosoyo formed the Kosovo Liberation Army (KLA) to fight for their interests. Serbs in Kosovo felt that the Serbian government in Belgrade had abandoned them and fought the KLA through Serbian militias. A low-level civil war brewed.

Ethnic conflict reached a peak in early 1999, and the Serbian government did little to prevent Serbian militias from driving ethnic Albanians from the province by force toward other nations in the region. An agreement was hammered out in Rambouillet, France, in February 1999, requiring Serbian and KLA forces to disarm. The United Nations would send in peacekeepers, and an election would determine the future status of Kosovo.

Serbian leader, Slobodan Milosevic, rejected the Rambouillet agreement, and the United States then began an air attack on military targets in both the Kosovo province and in the rest of Serbia to get his agreement. The bombing began on March 24, 1999, and lasted 73 days. On June 9, the Serbian forces withdrew from Kosovo. On June 28, 1999, the United Nations established a new peacekeeping force, KFOR, spots, much as it had in its prior 200-year history. Yet when those overseas commitments reflected neither clear self-interest nor a clear pursuit of American ideals, the American public and its political leaders remained reluctant to put troops at risk.

Some observers believed that the Vietnam syndrome still worked to limit American involvement. Despite the success of American participation in the liberation of Kuwait from the Iraqi invaders in 1991, the massive use of air power and the very light Coalition casualties suggested that the United States remained extremely cautious in its use of troops. As the polls had shown before Desert Storm, popular support for the war declined almost in proportion to the predicted number of casualties. Events in Somalia and in peacekeeping in the former Yugoslavia seemed to suggest that U.S. troops could be deployed only in very restricted ways.

composed of Russian, American, German, and French troops. KFOR occupied Kosovo and tried to keep Albanian and Serbian populations from killing each other. Many Albanian refugees returned home, and at the same time, many Serbs fled the province. It was a ragged peace.

In 1999, U.S. Marines were assigned to Kosovo in support of the NATO operation designed to provide peace and stability there. Here Marines escort Serbian detainees to the Kosovo-Serbian border where they were released to the Serbian authorities. *(Defense Imagery)*

Other aspects of the Persian Gulf War continued as living issues. The war had shown that the public's right to know through the news media often came in conflict with principles of national security and safety of soldiers in the field. Although print journalists and TV reporters were hungry for headlines and news scoops, the information disseminated in their stories could help an enemy and result in American casualties. Even though many in the media continued to insist that free access to information was a basic democratic right, more and more commentators came to accept the fact that sometimes publishing information could endanger the lives of American troops. On the other hand, that fact could be used to cover up mistakes and poor policy decisions. Finding the path between the goal of public information and national security remained difficult.

Another continuing debate arising from the Persian Gulf War centered on the endgame, as it played out in the last days of February 1991. Saddam Hussein remained in power through the decade, and many commentators questioned why he had not been removed from power in 1991, when General Schwarzkopf brought his troops to a halt and negotiated the cease-fire that ended the Persian Gulf War. Perhaps he should have gone on to Baghdad, many claimed, throwing out Hussein and establishing a friendlier government. But to argue that way 10 years later hardly seemed fair. In 1991, no advisers and very few outsiders thought going on to Baghdad was a good idea. Those who claimed, 10 or more years after the fact, that an opportunity to eliminate Hussein had been thrown away could only make that claim by forgetting the realities of 1991. At that time, public opinion and official policy in the U.S. and in the Muslim world dictated that Schwarzkopf liberate only Kuwait, not all or even part of Iraq.

As the United States reacted to further terrorist attacks in 2001, leading an air campaign and a new coalition to destroy the oppressive regime in Afghanistan that harbored Islamist terrorists, much of the legacy of the Persian Gulf War shaped the strategy and decisions. The Defense Department worked to keep American casualties to a minimum by first committing massive air power. President George W. Bush, the son of the Gulf War president, George H. W. Bush, made sure that little information was released that could interfere with operations. And every effort was made to track down and bring to justice the organizers and perpetrators of the terrorist crimes in hopes of limiting future repercussions.

An F-16CJ "Wild Weasel" pulls up to the refueling boom of a KC-135 Stratotanker over eastern Turkey as part of Operation Northern Watch, which enforced the no-fly zone over northern Iraq called for by the agreement that ended Operation Desert Storm. *(Defense Imagery)*

Future peacekeeping, future protection of American national interests, and further pursuit of American ideals on the world stage would all be influenced by the legacy of the Persian Gulf War of 1990–91.

In March 2003, the United States would lead another Coalition, consisting of a much smaller group of allied nations, in an attack on Iraq. In a short series of battles lasting from March 20 to May 1, 2003, the army of Saddam Hussein was defeated. However, the effort to establish a peaceful and democratic regime to replace that of Hussein continued against a violent resistance. The result was an extended war that dragged on into 2009 and 2010.

Saddam Hussein himself was captured by U.S. troops in December 2003 and executed by the new Iraqi government. Even after his death, former members of his Baath Party, radical Islamicists, and other dissidents continued an insurgency. The insurgents fought against both the new government and the U.S., British, and other foreign troops that sought to restore order to the country. But by spring 2010 it appeared that the combat phase for U.S. and Coalition forces in Iraq was near the end.

Glossary

air campaign   An attack without any troops on the ground, using land- and sea-based aircraft and missiles launched from land, air, or sea.

amphibious landing   A landing of troops and equipment from the sea in vehicles that travel through shallow water; some of these vehicles are able to travel over the beach. The U.S. Marines are specialists in this tactic.

antimissile missile   A missile intended as a defensive weapon to destroy incoming missiles. In the Persian Gulf War, the United States used the Patriot as an antimissile missile. (See Patriot.)

antipersonnel weapon   A weapon designed to kill troops rather than destroy equipment.

Arab Cooperation Council   Iraq, Jordan, Egypt, and Yemen formed this group in February 1989, with the goal of providing economic aid to poorer Arab countries. The United States approved, hoping the organization would limit Iraq's militarism.

armistice   An agreement between warring parties to cease fire either temporarily or permanently.

asymmetrical warfare   Warfare conducted by alternate means, such as guerrilla or terrorist attacks, in which the attacker has much smaller forces, not equal in strength with the defending party.

AWACS (airborne warning and control system)   A large aircraft designed to provide radar and communications backup to fighter and bomber aircraft.

Baath Party   Founded in Syria in the 1940s, the party offers a socialist vision of the future based on racial identity, bridging the religious differences among Arabic-speaking peoples. Saddam Hussein controls the Baath Party in Iraq.

barrel   A unit of measurement for crude oil, equal to 42 U.S. gallons.

berm   In construction, a berm is a raised earthen ridge. The Iraqi forces built large berms as fortifications or to protect a tank or other equipment.

Bradley   A U.S. Army infantry fighting vehicle, named after the popular World War II general Omar Bradley.

bunker   A concrete shelter against missile or bomb attacks, usually underground.

calutron   A device for the separation of uranium-235 from uranium-238 using electromagnets. Plans for calutrons that had been declassified in the United States were found by UN inspectors in Iraq and used in nuclear production facilities there.

cartel   A cartel is an organization designed to control prices for a product. The Organization of Petroleum Exporting Countries (OPEC) is a cartel that is made up of the oil ministers of many of the world's leading oil-producing nations.

casualties   In the case of battles, total casualties usually include those killed, wounded, or taken prisoner; when reported for an entire war, casualties may also include those who die in noncombat accidents.

chemical weapons   The term refers to various forms of poison gas, including nerve gas, chlorine, and phosgene. Chemical weapons have rarely been used in warfare since World War I, but Iraq had used them in its 1980–88 war with Iran.

cluster bomb   A canister that releases many grenade-size weapons, each exploding into deadly fragments.

commando   Highly trained forces used for quick and short-term special operations, such as landing behind enemy lines to destroy key facilities. The U.S. Navy Seals, the U.S. Army Rangers, and the British Special Armed Service (SAS) are commando units.

crude oil   Petroleum before it is refined into gasoline and other products.

cruise missile   A missile that is designed to fly at a relatively low level at extremely high speed, guided to its target by an internal computer. Cruise missiles can be ship-launched, ground-launched, or air-launched.

drone aircraft   A pilotless aircraft controlled from the ground and used to conduct aerial photography or to drop weapons over enemy positions.

feint   A false move, intended to convince the enemy that an advance is about to occur in one area to draw attention away from a genuine attack in another area.

flank   In military jargon, the sides of a force's position. The left flank of the enemy describes the side to the left from the viewpoint of the attacker. As a verb, to "flank" or "outflank" is to move around to attack on the side.

GBU (guided bomb unit) ordnance   A bomb that is laser-guided to its target. The GBU-10 carried 945 pounds of high explosive. The GBU-15 used either an infrared heat-seeking or video camera homing device. These were two types of smart bombs.

guest workers   Many countries extend temporary work permits to foreigners without granting them citizenship. Both Iraq and Kuwait employed hundreds of thousands of guest workers from Egypt, Pakistan, and India.

Gulf States   Kuwait, Qatar, Bahrain, United Arab Emirates, and Oman are all nations that border the Persian Gulf. Sometimes the term is also used to include Saudi Arabia.

Gulf War syndrome   Some U.S. troops who served in the Persian Gulf War later reported symptoms of a mysterious illness. Theories as to cause included breathing fumes from oil fires, exposure to radiation, chemical weapon residue from destroyed factories, and even the shots and pills issued to U.S. troops to prevent them from becoming ill from pathogens.

hardened   Specially reinforced, as when a shelter is built to withstand nearby blasts.

HARM (homing antiradar missile)   A missile designed to follow a radar beam to its source and destroy it. The British version of HARM is called ALARM.

human shield   Saddam Hussein announced in 1990 that many Europeans and Americans in Iraq were held at key military facilities. Air attacks on the facilities would kill these "human shields." Before Desert Storm, he released them.

Humvee (High Mobility Multipurpose Wheeled Vehicle, HMMWV)   A light all-terrain vehicle, larger and more rugged than the traditional jeep.

infrastructure   A nation's network of communication, utility, and transportation facilities, including electric utilities, telephone networks, radio and television stations, water supply and sewage, highways, bridges, railroads, and airports.

laser-guided   A bomb or missile equipped with a seeker device and movable fins so that it can "home in" on the reflection of a laser beam aimed at the target.

line charge   A device used to clear obstacles such as mine fields, consisting of a rocket that unreels a line of explosive charges over the obstacles.

logistics   The military science of organizing and transporting supplies and equipment needed for battle.

mobile launcher A vehicle that carries the mechanism for launching a weapon. Mobile cruise missiles are mounted on Transport-Erector-Launchers (TELs) so that they can be moved from place to place. Scuds mounted on TELs allowed quick removal so that retaliatory strikes would not destroy the crew or TEL.

MRE (meal-ready-to-eat) A packaged meal designed to provide basic nutrition for U.S. military but regarded by troops as "foul food."

nuclear proliferation The original five nations that developed nuclear weapons (United States, Soviet Union, Britain, France, and China) sought to prevent the spread or proliferation of weapons to other countries. Iraq appeared ready to build a nuclear weapon in 1990.

OAPEC (Organization of Arab Petroleum Exporting Countries) OAPEC is a group within OPEC.

OPEC (Organization of Petroleum Exporting Countries) A cartel that tries to control the world price of crude oil.

Osiraq reactor The nuclear reactor at Tuwaitha, outside of Baghdad, Iraq, which was used for nuclear research. Israel launched a destructive air raid on Osiraq on June 8, 1981.

Patriot A surface-to-air missile originally designed as an antiaircraft missile but adapted in the Persian Gulf War to intercept incoming enemy missiles. As a system, the Patriot involves a command station, a radar unit, computers, and eight to 16 launchers, each with four Patriot missiles.

POW (prisoner of war) When combatant troops of an enemy are captured, they become prisoners of war. The term does not apply to civilians of an enemy power, who are usually returned or repatriated to their home country unless they have engaged in hostilities. In those cases, they can be tried and, if found guilty, punished.

propaganda Originally, any information released or "propagated." The term refers to biased or manufactured information designed by a government or political group to sway opinion.

Ramadan In the Muslim calendar, Ramadan is the ninth month of the year and is regarded as a holy period for prayer, reading the Koran, and daytime fasting. In 1991, Ramadan officially began on March 17.

refugees People who flee war zones or political oppression are refugees. An estimated 400,000 of Kuwait's 800,000 citizens fled as refugees, as did more than 1 million Kurds in Northern Iraq.

sanction A punitive measure adopted by one or more nations against a nation regarded as violating international law. It usually involves the prohibition of trade, transportation, and other contacts with the nation.

scramble   The takeoff of one or more aircraft for a sortie.

Scud   A missile developed by the Soviet Union and based on the German V-2 rocket of World War II. The Iraqis modified Scud missiles by welding together two SS-1 (surface-to-surface, type 1) missiles provided by the Soviet Union, reputedly increasing their range to more than 300 miles. In 1990, Iraq had an estimated 65 Scud missiles.

SLAM (Standoff Land Attack Missile)   A missile used against surface targets and usually deployed from carrier-based aircraft.

smart bombs   Several types of weapons that could be precisely guided or directed to targets. Costing more than $50,000 apiece, they were used sparingly during the Persian Gulf War on high-value targets such as specific office buildings and military facilities. (See GBU.)

sortie   An individual aircraft flight, from takeoff through landing.

Stealth fighter/bomber   U.S. aircraft designed with special materials and with angular surfaces to evade radar. In the Gulf War, there were two such planes, the F-117A Nighthawk fighter-bomber, called by pilots the "Wobbly Goblin," and the B-2 bomber.

Tomahawk   A sea-launched cruise missile used by the U.S. Navy for the first time in warfare during the Persian Gulf War. The missile is guided by an internal computer that follows the terrain. Although usually accurate to a few meters, several Tomahawk missiles hit unintended targets during the Persian Gulf War.

UNSCOM (United Nations Special Commission)   Commission that was established to conduct inspections to ensure that Iraq did not develop weapons of mass destruction.

Vietnam syndrome   Following the Vietnam War, the American public resisted the use of U.S. troops overseas. American and foreign leaders believed the syndrome would prevent any sustained use of military force in future situations.

Warthog   The informal name for the A-10 Thunderbolt, a large, slow, and ugly aircraft used in destroying tanks and other armored vehicles.

weapons of mass destruction (WMDs)   These weapons include nuclear and thermonuclear bombs and missiles, poison gas, and biological weapons that spread diseases.

Further Reading

BOOKS

Adams, James. *Bull's Eye: The Assassination and Life of the Supergun Inventor Gerald Bull.* New York: Times Books, 1992.

Atkinson, Rick. *Crusade: The Untold Story of the Persian Gulf War.* New York: Mariner Books, 1994.

Baker, James. *The Politics of Diplomacy: Revolution, War and Peace, 1989–1992.* New York: G. P. Putnam's Sons, 1995.

Benson, Nicholas. *Rat's Tales: The Staffordshire Regiment at War in the Gulf.* London: Brassey's, 1993.

Bethke, Jean. *But Was It Just?: Reflections on the Morality of the Persian Gulf War.* New York: Galilee Trade Press, 1992.

Bin, Alberto, Richard Hill, and Archer Jones. *Desert Storm: A Forgotten War.* Westport, Conn.: Praeger, 1998.

Blackwell, James. *Thunder in the Desert: The Strategy and Tactics of the Persian Gulf War.* New York: Bantam Books, 1991.

Blair, John M. *The Control of Oil.* New York: Vintage Books, 1978.

Bodansky, Yossef. *Bin Laden: The Man Who Declared War on America.* New York: Prima, 2001.

Bourque, Stephan Alan, and John W. Burdan. *The Road to Safwan: The 1st Squadron, 4th Cavalry in the 1991 Persian Gulf War.* Denton: University of North Texas Press, 2007.

Bush, George H. W., and Brent Scowcroft. *A World Transformed.* New York: Alfred Knopf, 1998.

Carhart, Tom. *Iron Soldiers: How America's 1st Armored Division Crushed Iraq's Elite Republican Guard.* New York: Pocket Books, 1994.

Cordesman, Anthony. *The Gulf and the Search for Strategic Stability.* Boulder, Colo.: Westview Press, 1984.

Falk, Richard. *Revolutionaries and Functionaries: The Dual Face of Terrorism.* New York: E. P. Dutton, 1980.

Finlan, Alastair. *The Gulf War 1991.* New York: Routledge, 2003.

Freedman, Lawrence, and Efraim Karsh. *The Gulf Conflict, 1990–1991: Diplomacy and War in the New World Order.* Princeton, N.J.: Princeton University Press, 1993.

Friedman, Norman. *Desert Victory: The War for Kuwait.* Annapolis, Md.: United States Naval Institute, 1992.

Friedrich, Otto, ed. *Desert Storm: The War in the Persian Gulf.* Boston: Little, Brown, 1991.

Fromkin, David. *A Peace to End All Peace: Creating the Modern Middle East, 1914–1922.* New York: Henry Holt, 1989.

Gordon, Michael R., and Bernard E. Trainor. *The General's War: The Inside Story of the Conflict in the Gulf.* Boston: Little, Brown, 1995.

Hallion, Richard P. *Storm over Iraq: Air Power and the Gulf War.* Washington, D.C.: Smithsonian Institution Press, 1992.

Head, William, and Earl H. Tilford. *The Eagle in the Desert: Looking Back on U.S. Involvement in the Persian Gulf War.* New York: Praeger 1996.

Hiro, Dilip. *Desert Shield to Desert Storm: The Second Gulf War.* New York: Routledge Press, 1992.

———. *Holy Wars: The Rise of Islamic Fundamentalism.* New York: Routledge Press, 1989.

Lacey, Robert. *The Kingdom: Arabia and the House of Sa'ud.* New York: Random House, 1987.

McKinnon, Dan. *Bullseye Iraq.* New York: Berkley Books, 1988.

McNab, Andy. *Bravo Two Zero.* London: Corgi, 1994.

Miller, Judith, and Laurie Mylroie. *Saddam Hussein and the Crisis in the Gulf.* New York: Random House, 1990.

Morrison, David E. *Television and the Gulf War.* London: John Libbey, 1992.

Newell, Clayton R. *The A to Z of the Persian Gulf War 1990–1991.* Lanham, Md.: Scarecrow Press, 2007.

Nye, Joseph S., Jr., and Roger K. Smith, eds. *After the Storm: Lessons from the Gulf War.* Lanham, Md.: Aspen Institute and Madison Books, 1992.

Powell, Colin, with Joseph Persico. *My American Journey.* New York: Ballantine, 1995.

Putney, Diane Therese. *Airpower Advantage: Planning the Gulf War Air Campaign, 1989–1991.* Washington, D.C.: Department of the Air Force, 2005.

Pyle, Richard. *Schwarzkopf in His Own Words: The Man, The Mission, The Triumph.* New York: Signet, 1991.

Ritter, Scott. *Endgame: Solving the Iraq Problem—Once and For All.* New York: Simon and Schuster, 1999.

Roth, David. *Sacred Honor: Colin Powell, The Inside Account of His Life and Triumphs.* New York: HarperCollins, 1993.

Sasson, Jean P. *The Rape of Kuwait: The True Story of Iraqi Atrocities Against a Civilian Population.* New York: Knightsbridge, 1991.

Sifry, Micah L., and Christopher Cerf. *The Gulf War Reader: History, Documents, Opinion.* New York: Random House, 1991.

Summers, Harry G. *On Strategy II: A Critical Analysis of the Gulf War.* New York: Dell, 1992.

Thompson, Phillip. *Into the Storm: A U.S. Marine in the Persian Gulf War.* Jefferson, N.C.: McFarland, 2001.

Woodward, Bob. *The Commanders.* New York: Simon and Schuster, 1991.

ARTICLES

Adelman, M. A. "After the Gulf War: Oil Fallacies." *Foreign Policy* 82 (1991): 3–16.

Ajami, Fouad. "The Summer of Arab Discontent." *Foreign Affairs* 69 (1990/91): 1–20.

Albright, David, and Mark Hibbs. "Iraq's Bomb: Blueprints and Artifacts." *Bulletin of the Atomic Scientists,* January/February 1992, pp. 30–40.

———. "Iraq's Nuclear Hide and Seek." *Bulletin of the Atomic Scientists,* September 1991, pp. 14–23.

Arkin, William M. "U.S. Nukes in the Gulf." *The Nation,* December 31, 1990, pp. 834–836.

Brzezinski, Zbigniew. "Selective Global Commitment." *Foreign Affairs* 70 (1991): 1–20.

Krauthammer, Charles. "The Unipolar Moment." *Foreign Affairs* 70 (1991): 23–33.

MacLeod, Scott. "In the Wake of Desert Storm." *The New York Review of Books,* March 7, 1991, pp. 6–9.

Rodman, Peter W. "Middle East Diplomacy after the Gulf War." *Foreign Affairs* 70 (1991): 1–18.

"The Signals That Were Sent—and the One That Wasn't." *The Economist,* September 29, 1990, pp. 19–22.

Warner, Frederick. "The Environmental Consequences of the Gulf War." *Environment* 33 (1991): 6–9.

WEB SITES

The History Guy. URL: www.historyguy.com/GulfWar.html

Frontline: The Gulf War. URL: www.pbs.org/wgbh/pages/frontline/gulf/

About dot com: American History—The Gulf War. URL: http://americanhistory.about.com/od/persiangulfwar/Persian_Gulf_Wars.htm

PERSIAN GULF WAR, 1990–1991: Desert Shield/Desert Storm (Air Force Official site). URL: www.au.af.mil/au/aul/bibs/pgwar/pgwrtc.htm

Index

Page numbers in *italic* indicate a photograph. Page numbers followed by *m* indicate maps. Page numbers followed by *g* indicate glossary entries. Page numbers in **boldface** indicate box features.